ORIGINS OF
CROW AGENCIES
IN MONTANA

ORIGINS OF
CROW AGENCIES
IN MONTANA

TRANSITIONING BEYOND THE BUFFALO

PATTY MOLINARO

Foreword by Bill Yellowtail, Crow statesman & educator

THE
History
PRESS

Published by The History Press
Charleston, SC
www.historypress.com

First published 2024

Manufactured in the United States

ISBN 9781467156905

Library of Congress Control Number: 2023950636

CONTENTS

FOREWORD

And then there were no buffalo.

H ence to regret and despair? Or shall we choose to be affirmative—
make the best of our possibilities, adjust, pursue our vision? Just
as we always have. By this we have eternally guarded the Crow
Heartland, the Crow heart.

Not just to survive or endure, but to thrive. Thrivance, we call it nowadays.

We treasure our values and shall ensure that they, too, prosper. Clan.
Family. Ceremony. Language. Art form. Spirituality. Our material conditions
might have to adapt, but Crow identity and culture shall thrive.

In a series of negotiated treaties and agreements, the Crow Indians
bargained hard for terms advantageous to their own agenda. They reserved
for their exclusive possession and use the heart of their ancestral territory. In
the Fort Laramie Treaty of 1868, that reserved heartland encompassed the
Absaroka, Beartooth, Pryor, Big Horn and Crazy Mountains regions.

The 1868 treaty called for installation of an "agency" (in government
parlance) for purposes of serving Crow interests and needs during that time
of transition. Fort Parker was constructed in 1869 and later relocated to the
newly built Absaroka Agency, established in 1875. Subsequently, the agency
moved to its current location at Crow Agency, Montana, in 1884.

The Absaroka Agency period marked the pivot point of Crow transition
from the old buffalo days to an unknown future. Unknown, perhaps, but
always anticipated and planned for by the forceful, visionary leaders of the

Crow Nation. Sits in the Middle of the Land. Iron Bull. Pretty Eagle. Medicine Crow. The young Plenty Coups, whose prescience was received on a peak in the Crazy Mountains. Baacheeit'che, Good Men worthy of leadership.

Thus emerged the challenges opened at the outset of this foreword. They are persistent questions, always before us, then and now. By those questions we perpetually strive for thrivance, culturally, economically, humanly.

Origins of Crow Agencies in Montana: Transitioning Beyond the Buffalo serves to remind us of the settings, conditions, characters and dynamics leading up to and through the early agency era. If some of us have forgotten, now we will appreciate once again this critical milestone of our heritage.

—Bill Yellowtail, prominent figure in the Crow Tribe, former Montana State Senator, legislator and frequent lecturer on the history of his people

ACKNOWLEDGEMENTS

I am forever grateful for the support, expertise and encouragement of those who contributed to this publication, A–Z:

Aaron Brien
Alden Big Man
Arzelee Drown
Bill Yellowtail
Bob Hermstad
Casey Olsen
Crystal Alegria
Daniel Keller
Elias Goes Ahead (in memoriam)
Harlan Conroy
Linda Dutcher
Lorrie Henri Koski
Mardell Plainfeather Hogan
Marsha Fulton
Peggy Welliever
Ralph and Marlene Saunders
Shane Doyle
Steve Aaberg
Tim McCleary
Further thanks to:

Acknowledgements

Becca Kohl, Montana Historical Society
Daisy Njoku, Smithsonian, NAA
Eileen Wright, Montana State University, Billings, Montana
Jeff Malcomson, Montana Historical Society
Nathan Sowry, NMAI
Penny Redli, Museum of the Beartooths, Columbus, Montana
Richard Tritt, Cumberland County Historical Society, Carlisle
Artie Crisp, Abigail Fleming and the crew at The History Press

1

CHILDREN OF THE LARGE BEAKED BIRD

Oral accounts and archaeological findings indicate a migration of ancestral Crow and Hidatsa peoples from the Midwest. Near present-day Spirit (Devils) Lake, North Dakota, two leaders, No Intestines (also called No Vitals) and Red Scout, both fasted, receiving instruction and guidance for their future. Cultivation of corn was to sustain the peoples in settlements near suitable river bottoms in Red Scout's vision. His people became the historic Hidatsa. No Intestines's vision foresaw the Sacred Tobacco plant and its proper usage would perpetuate his followers in a large, beautiful homeland.[1] Eventually, his followers located tobacco growing in the Big Horn Mountains of present-day Montana and Wyoming. Thus, his peoples became the historic Crow, who evolved into three political divisions: the Mountain Crow, who were the largest division and first to enter Wyoming-Montana regions; the River Crow, who left the Hidatsa proper over a dispute involving a buffalo stomach; and Kicked In The Bellies, a derivative of the Mountain Crow that splintered from the group.[2] The Kicked In The Bellies were so named after a swift lesson involving both hooves from of a new acquisition called the horse.[3]

The Mountain Crow ranged from the present-day Montana-Wyoming border to the eastern Powder River country and west toward present-day Livingston, Montana. River Crow extended from the Yellowstone River to north along the Milk River, and Kicked In The Bellies stretched from the Big Horn Mountains to central Wyoming's Wind River Range.

"Sharp People" was the collective name other tribes called these bands, "implying that they were as crafty and alert as the bird, 'absa' (probably the raven)." Sharp People, imitated in sign language by flapping arms that represented bird's wings, probably led to the erroneous translation of "Crow" by early Euro American traders.[4]

Perhaps not the Crow people's first encounter with trappers and traders, but a notable one, was François Larocque. On June 25, 1805, near the confluence of the Missouri and Knife Rivers, Larocque witnessed and recorded a procession of some 654 Crow men wearing bright buckskin clothing, carrying painted rawhide shields, sitting astride their prized ponies. It was he who contributed to their name *gens de corbeaux* (People of the Crow), by which the Euro-American world came to know them.[5] Apsáalooke/ Apsaarooke[6] is the name Crow people of present-day southeastern Montana formally call themselves. This translates from the Hidatsa tribal language as "Children of the Large Beaked Bird."[7]

Distinguished Crow Indians, 1861/1869, George Catlin. *Paul Mellon Collection, National Gallery of Art, Washington, D.C.*

Tintypes of Robert Meldrum and Medicine Tree. *P08166, NMAI.AC.386.*

Early contact with the traders provided the Crow experience serving as the middleman, bringing Euro-American goods into the Northern Rockies from trading outposts along the Missouri River. Such relations, contact and negotiations also provided a sample of the new world coming.[8]

One such trade associate was Robert Meldrum, pictured here. By the late 1820s, the Scottish immigrant was working in the fur trade industry. In 1833, the American Fur Company hired him as a company liaison with the Crow and posted Meldrum along various trading locations along the Yellowstone and Upper Missouri Rivers. The Plains tribes brought various furs there to be traded for guns, ammunition, clothing, beads and other goods. Meldrum also learned to speak the Crow language and served as an interpreter between the tribe and U.S. government.

TREATIES AND PEACE COMMISSIONS

Conceived decades after trading and white contact, the Crow negotiated their first treaty, the so-called Friendship Treaty, with the United States in 1825. Within this treaty, the main clause called for the Crow and other western tribes to recognize the supremacy of the U.S. government and remain loyal to it and its liscened traders. In return, the government vowed protection from dishonest traders and the return of stolen horses and personal possessions that might be pilfered from them in the future. The treaty also implied a set of territory boundaries for members of all tribes who signed.[9]

A second treaty process with western Native tribes and government officials was prompted by safety concerns for increasing migrant movement across the plains. In 1851 the United States appropriated $100,000 to cover the costs of meeting with nearly ten thousand Crow, Sioux, Cheyenne, Arapaho, Shoshone, Arikara and Assiniboine who gathered near Fort Laramie, Wyoming. Due to overcrowding numbers, the council relocated forty miles east to Horse Creek. Within a week, the newly created Fort Laramie Treaty of 1851 ensured safe passage for white travelers, secured pledges among tribal leaders to remain peaceful among themselves and provided the right for the United States to lay out roads and establish miliary posts in Indian territory. The United States also agreed to pay each signatory tribe $50,000 in annuities annually for fifty years, later reduced to ten years, with another five, discretionary. The treaty went on to define tribal territories (reservations were not yet established) as represented by the 1851 map drawn by treaty participant Jesuit Father Pierre DeSmet. For the Crow peoples, represented by their leader Big Robber and interpreter Robert Meldrum, this meant the retention of their present domain and hunting grounds.[10]

Pierre-Jean DeSmet, *Map of the upper Great Plains and Rocky Mountains region, 1851. loc.gov/resource/g4050.ct000883.*

Warfare

Indian and immigrant conflict in the West escalated with the 1864 discovery of gold in Montana. Leading to the gold camps was the newly blazed Bozeman Trail. It coursed through the heart of Crow country, triggering skirmishes between prospectors and hostile tribes, primarily the Lakota Sioux, who claimed the Crow lands as their own. The conflicts prompted the U.S. miliary to construct three protective army posts along the trail: Forts Reno, Phil Kearny and C.F. Smith. Soon the posts were in a constant siege of attack under the Sioux leadership of Red Cloud and Crazy Horse, who demanded closure of the posts. The Crow rejected joining the Sioux in these forays denoted as "Red Cloud's War," instead pledging loyalty to the United States with hopes of regaining their lost hunting grounds.[11]

A severe blow to the military occurred at Fort Phil Kearny on December 21, 1866, when a detachment of eighty troops led by Captain William J. Fetterman was annihilated by Sioux and Cheyenne warriors. This prompted government investigations with the resulting Fetterman and Doolittle Reports. The latter, named after chairman Senator James R. Doolittle of Wisconsin, found worsening conditions among tribes ascribable to the aggressions of "lawless white men," the loss of hunting grounds and abuse and fraud within the government system.[12]

In 1867, Congress faced a critical stage in the history of the country. The Senate debated whether the government should attempt to assimilate, concentrate or exterminate the Indians. When the contentious argument turned to the high price of fighting "hostile" Indians, Senator John B. Henderson of Missouri stood and forcefully stated, "If we can make peace with the Indians, we had better do it."[13] Ultimately, a bill was authorized on July 20, 1867, giving President Andrew Johnson authority to select a Peace Commission on the premise that wars were costly. Although assimilation (Indian integration) was controversial, Indians were not to impede westward expansion but rather accept the march of integration into mainstream society. The appointed seven-man commission faced the task of establishing permanent peace and securing rights to overland routes, in particular for railroads. Congress believed peace could best be achieved by persuading the Indians to abandon their nomadic hunting lifestyles in exchange for reservation life supported through agricultural pursuits.[14]

Fort Laramie, Wyoming Territory, was the designated meeting location for tribes and peace commissioners. Many tribes, including the Arapaho, Arikara, Assiniboine, Cheyenne, Crow, Gros Ventre, Mandan, Shoshone and

Sioux Nations, traveled long distances to gather and hear the government's terms. Although the Crow were hoping to gather at Fort Phil Kearny,[15] they instead twice journeyed the extra miles to Fort Laramie, in the fall of 1867 and spring of 1868.

Joining the Peace Commission was photographer Alexander Gardner, former associate of the acclaimed Civil War photographer Mathew Brady. Gardner was recruited by Christopher C. Augur, a former Civil War officer with an interest in photo documentation. As a result, Augur received copies of Gardner's work, thus providing us a visual glimpse of the occasions. Among the notable photographs is one of a special agent to the Crow, Dr.

Above: Crow Indian family on the march. *Edward E. Ayer Digital Collection (Newberry Library)* *NL001075.*

Opposite, top: Group about Fort Laramie. *Edward E. Ayer Digital Collection (Newberry Library)* *NL001165.*

Opposite, bottom: Bear's Claw. *Edward E. Ayer Digital Collection (Newberry Library) NL001079.*

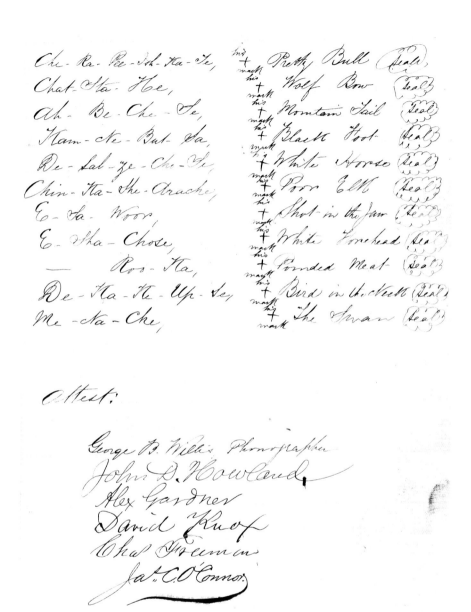

Che - Ra - Pee - Ish - Ha - Te,
Chat - Sta - Hee,
Ah - Be - Che - Se,
Kam - Ne - But - Sa,
De - Sal - ze - Che - Se,
Chin - Ha - She - Arache,
E - Sa - Woos,
E - Sha - Chose,
——— Ros - Ha,
De - Ha - He - Up - Se,
Me - Na - Che,

his + mark Pretty Bull (Seal)
his + mark Wolf Bow (Seal)
his + mark Mountain Tail (Seal)
his + mark Black Foot (Seal)
his + mark White Horse (Seal)
his + mark Poor Elk (Seal)
his + mark Shot in the Jaw (Seal)
his + mark White Forehead (Seal)
his + mark Pounded Meat (Seal)
his + mark Bird in the Neck (Seal)
his + mark The Swan (Seal)

Attest:

George B. Willis Photographer
John D. Howland
Alex Gardner
David Knox
Chas Freeman
Jas. C. O'Connor

Ratified Indian Treaty—Fort Laramie, Dakota Territory, May 7, 1868. *catalog.archives.gov/id/179035469.*

H.M. Mathews, standing next to the Mountain Crow leaders (*left to right*): Mountain Tail, Pounded Meat, Blackfoot, Winking Eye, White Fawn, White Horse, Poor Elk, Shot in the Jaw, Crow and Pretty Bull.

Riding to Laramie on a mule, favored due to their stamina, is participant Bear's Tooth (also called Bear's Claw). He is prepared with his Navajo chief blanket behind him, a major trade item, and a bow and quiver case on his back.[16] During the two-day November council, he arose and offered his pipe four times, then pleaded with the commissioners for the welfare of the Crow peoples. He also spoke of concerns with the Sioux and mistreatment by the whites. He acknowledged the troubling times: "Father, Father, the Great Spirit made us all, but he put the red man in the centre [*sic*] surrounded by the whites. Ah, my heart is full and sad." Bear's Tooth refused the government's plan for the Crow to farm and raise cattle. "I have been raised on buffalo meat, and left to move my camp where I like— to roam over the prairies at will." Concluding his speech, he turned and gave his pair of moccasins to Commissioner Nathanial G. Taylor to "keep your feet warm."[17] This promoted Blackfoot, "a Crow warrior of gigantic stature," to rise and place a buffalo robe on the shoulders of Taylor "as a token of brotherhood."[18]

Blackfoot then spoke of Crow faithfulness to the whites and government failure to fulfill annuities owed under terms of the 1851 treaty. "Pay first what you owe us," he insisted, before speaking of another agreement. Wolf Bow, the River Crow leader, last to speak, reiterated the tribe ought to be allowed to live in their traditional manner.[19] A treaty was presented for their signature, but since demands by both the Crow and Sioux to abandon the forts along the Bozeman Trail had not been accomplished, they rejected signing but agreed to meet the following spring.[20]

Thus, in May, the Crow returned to this outpost on the Laramie River, fringed with "stunted cottonwoods, a few willows, flaunting sunflowers and long prairie grasses."[21] They found Sioux, Cheyenne and Arapaho representatives, but Red Cloud and a few strongholds refused to come until the forts were actually abandoned. However, after minimal discussion on May 7, 1868, eleven Crow leaders signed the treaty.[22] The only River Crow who consented to sign was Wolf Bow.[23]

The eight-page Treaty of Fort Laramie (1868) would drastically, and forever, change tribal life.[24]

2

FORT PARKER

The treaty of 1868 reduced Crow domain from over 38 million to 8 million acres, with given reservation boundaries. It also outlined directives to transition the Crow from traditional lifestyles to permanent tribal settlement on their reservation, including the distribution of yearly annuity goods of clothing and mandated education for children aged six to sixteen. Although the Crow were self-reliant and self-sufficient, the document specified farming as the means of reinventing themselves as productive citizens of the United States. To this end, provisions for farming instruction—and enticements of $100 worth of seeds, implements and "one good American cow, and one well-broken pair of American oxen"—would be provided to any family or lodge that settled and farmed on the reservation. A recorded tract of 320 reservation acres was promised to potential farmers.[25] Gifts of $500 a year were assured to ten persons growing the best crops for three consecutive years.

THE CROW'S FIRST AGENCY

Article 111 specified an agency was to be established within the reservation and construction of a warehouse as well as residences for the agent, physician, carpenter, blacksmith, farmer, miller and engineer. It called also for a school house or mission house and a good steam-powered circular sawmill to grind flour and make shingles. The treaty stated the Crow's first agency site should be constructed on the south side of the Yellowstone River, near Otter Creek,[26]

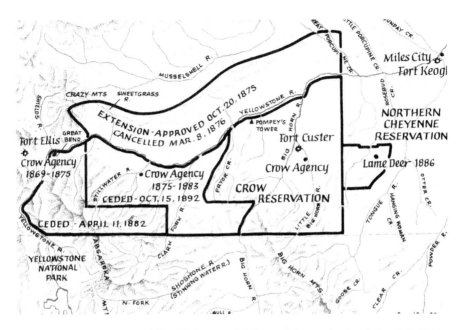

Plainsmen of the Yellowstone by Mark H. Brown. *G.P. Putnam's Sons, an imprint of Penguin Publishing Group, a division of Penguin Random House LLC.*

leading to confusion, as there were "three creeks called by that name."[27] A preferable location was found near the Shields River. However, a selection was made near the mouth of what would be called Mission Creek, ten miles from present-day Livingston, Montana, and thirty-five miles from the military post, Fort Ellis. The site lacked adequate timber, had poor access, was said to be "infested with war parties" and rumored to contain "rich gold diggings." Adding to the poor prospects, the Crow objected the location would interfere with their best buffalo hunting grounds.[28]

Anticipated as bastions of the future, the agency would not serve as military fort but rather as the headquarters for Crow annuity and provision distributions, their farming instruction, schooling and trading purposes. Housed here were the employees and a U.S. government agent charged with following orders to assist and encourage the Crow tribe to set aside all that was traditional and familiar for new ways.

Captain Erskine M. Camp was appointed as the Crow's first Indian agent. However, Bozeman merchant Leander M. Black was hired while Camp was delayed for nearly ten weeks due to lack of transportation near Fort Benton, Montana Territory. In accordance with treaty specifications and before the onset of winter in 1869, Black and crew constructed out of cottonwood a warehouse; homes for the physician, engineer, blacksmith, carpenter, farmer and miller; and a building to be used as a schoolhouse.[29]

The agency was called Fort Parker, likely named for Ely S. Parker, then commissioner of Indian affairs in Washington, but was often called the "Mission" Agency. It is probable Fort Parker was called the Mission Agency after the pattern of early Indian tribes who described Christian outposts as "missions." The adjacent Mission Creek is still the proper name for the waterway.[30]

Camp finally arrived at Fort Parker in November 1869. Among his first actions was plowing and cultivating ground for farming purposes. The following spring, more land was broken with vegetables and experimental grains seeded. A heavy frost killed most. Despite efforts to encourage farming practices, only one Crow among the whole tribe expressed an interest to remain at the agency to farm, Wolf Bow, the second to sign the Fort Laramie Treaty of 1868. Agent Erskine Camp built him a house. Hopeful tribal members would see the benefits and wish to follow his example, he optimistically remarked, "A beginning is everything."[31] Wolf Bow was later awarded one cow and two broke oxen as detailed in Article 9 of the 1868 treaty.[32] Camp soon faced a recurring barrier to settling the Crow, incessant attacks and raids on them and the agency by hostile tribes, predominately Lakota Sioux. He suggested arming the Crow for the protection of all.[33]

Fort Parker, the Mission Agency

Several accounts provide visual details about Fort Parker, pictured on the following page. By August 1870, reports describe the agency consisting of a "warehouse, agency building, houses for physician, engineer, blacksmith, carpenter, farmer, and miller, and a building to be used as a school-room." The agency building or "mission-house" itself became housing for thirteen men of Company A, Seventh Infantry, detailed to protect the compound. A pair of twelve-pound howitzers mounted on bastions and placed crosswise from each enforced the means.[34] The following year, Fort Parker, pictured in 1871, was described as "three corner buildings, three rooms each, 15 feet square; one used as resident for the agent, one as hospital and quarters for surgeon." The third sufficed as mission house. The compound also contained two forty-five-by-fifteen-foot warehouses.

A news correspondent from the *Bozeman Avant Courier* described the agency in 1872 as consisting of "a fort about 200 ft. square built, of sawed timbers; with two bastions….Outside the fort are twenty-two double houses (24 x 16 ft.)[35] built of adobe with two fire-places in each, which make very comfortable houses for the Indians. The houses are built equal distance from each other, on either side of an avenue one hundred feet in width and about four hundred yards long."[36] Another visitor observed the agency resembled "a small barrack" complete with trader's store, church and schoolhouse. He found the employees, agent and "missionary" quarters "comfortable."[37]

AGENT FELLOWS D. PEASE

More than likely due to reaction to the horrific army massacre of the Piegan Indians led by Major Eugene Baker on January 23, 1870, there was a change in government Indian strategy.[38] The Crow Reservation, like others, was

Fort Parker. *Montana Historical Society (MHS)-955-902.*

restored to the control of the Indian Office, thus barring army officers from filling civil positions. This triggered the replacement of Captain Camp with Fellows D. Pease as the new Crow agent on November 14, 1870.[39]

Pease, a native Pennsylvanian, moved at an early age to New York and then Wisconsin. Here, in his early teens, he began trade with the Chippewa Indians and at age nineteen was involved with the survey of the Wisconsin-Minnesota border. Pease was in Montana Territory by 1856, employed as a scout for General Sully and later General Harney. He next became involved in the fur trade, learning sign language as well as becoming conversant in Crow. In 1859, he married Margaret Wallace, of Crow and Scottish descent. The commissioner of Indian affairs appointed him as a special Indian agent in 1867, and three years later Pease became the Crow agent at Fort Parker.[40]

The new agent was quick to discern the many problems and threats the Crow would face and set the tone early; he was a man of business. On his first day, he discovered the only tribal provisions his predecessor left him were twenty-six sacks of flour and two sacks of sugar.[41] Other government property consisted of "nine head of oxen, one cow, one horse and one pair of mules." "Hence," he reported, "I commenced here with little," and chided the Montana superintendent of Indian affairs about the treatment of the Crow, "peaceable and well disposed," who deserved better.[42] He also noted twenty families of mixed blood who by tribal "consent and wishes," were associated to the agency under the auspices of Article 2 and 9 of the 1868 treaty. "They have mostly located homesteads, and gone to work." Pease found they encouraged farming efforts by others and would assist them "to the extent" of his power and recommended a survey of the reservation to assist in locating and recording homesteads.[43]

With a hint of sorrow, Pease also reported a serious issue occurring in the southwestern mountainous region of the Crow Reservation. Miners were busily staking and mining claims in Emigrant, Bear and numerous other gulches. Many of the claims, "quite successful," were established prior to the establishment of the Crow Reservation in 1868. Though the treaty of 1868 allocated

Fellows D. Pease. *MHS 944.301.*

this as Crow country, it was already home to one hundred miners[44] who claimed their mining priority rights.[45] Though they were illegally on the reservation, Pease discovered there were "hundreds" moving in with a "great thirst for gold." Their roaming the reservation created a "source of great anxiety and trouble" to the Crow. He reflected that a few years earlier the valleys had "scarcely been marked by the foot-prints of white men" and predicted the future did not bode well for the Crow. He found the subject "too melancholy to dwell upon," for past experience had shown it "almost impossible for the Government to protect the Indians" in their treaty rights. Due to lack of precise boundaries and the mountainous terrain, Pease predicted removing the miners would be "very difficult." Selling "this portion of the Crow county is almost the only way to settle the matter satisfactorily to all parties," he concluded. To this end, Pease proposed the Crow visit Washington to discuss the matter. Hearing "wonderful" stories of the Sioux leader Red Cloud's visit and what "the party saw and heard and how well they were treated, has given the Crow quite an anxiety to go," he exclaimed.[46]

The second contention the agent and Crow faced, the coming Northern Pacific Railroad, was a movement that began in 1864. Such a link binding east to west was in the works after President Abraham Lincoln signed a charter on July 2 for a railroad spanning from Lake Superior to the Puget Sound in Washington. Construction was delayed until 1869, when financial backing was procured. While the Northern Pacific Railroad was building across the prairies east of the Missouri, survey crews worked out the route between the Missouri Crossing at Bismarck, North Dakota and the Bozeman Pass in Montana Territory. Railroad charters called for grants of land extending for twenty miles on either side of the proposed rail bed, some of which would traverse the Crow Reservation set aside by the treaty of 1868.[47] In anticipation of the Northern Pacific Railroad, mining activity increased, prompting the Crow to "bitterly" protest the miners' presence, which disrupted wild game and hunting prospects. Pease warned that if measures were not taken to keep the miners off, "serious trouble" would erupt.[48]

A third issue facing the Crow was the incessant raiding on them at or near Fort Parker, predominantly by the Lakota Sioux.

The Sioux

Sioux warring with the Crow was a long-standing matter noted the late historian Robert Utley.[49] The first recorded hostility between the tribes occurred around 1785 in the Black Hills, which the Crow controlled during this time. The scuffle was over an attempt by a pair of Sioux to take a Crow horse. They were discovered and killed. This period also marked the beginning of a strong Sioux presence in the Northern Plains.[50]

Bands of Lakota Sioux "routinely came to Crow county on horse-capturing or coup-counting raids." They had been driven by "westward expansion," and as a result conflicts "became more frequent and more hostile in nature."[51]

Despite the fact the Sioux were given their own reservation in present-day South Dakota, they directed endless hostilities toward the Crow at Fort Parker. This greatly hindered agents' attempts to guide the Crow into mainstream society. A frustrated Agent Pease seethed on account of the Crow Reservation "overrun by war parties of Sioux Indians" it was "almost impossible" for them "to feel any degree of safety for themselves or property."[52] Along with mining and railroad complications, these further issues stirred a sense of urgency for the government to negotiate with the Crow.

One incident of raiding by the Sioux near Fort Parker occurred on September 21, 1872. A range of nearly one hundred warriors crossed paths with Dr. John Frost. Frost, a former Union surgeon, had left Fort Parker to tend to a patient and was on his way home. Accompanying him were two Indian women and a baby, relatives of his wife. The Sioux killed all four. Frost left behind Strong Face, his wife, of mixed Spanish and Piegan blood, and a seven-month-old son. Frost was held in high esteem by the Crow, so in appreciation, Chief Blackfoot adopted his widow and child into the Crow Tribe. The boy, also called John Frost, eventually became a Baptist minister.

Felix Brunot

Montana delegates began setting their own plans in motion to resolve Crow issues by introducing a House Resolution on March 12, 1872, authorizing the secretary of the interior to negotiate a land "surrender" with the tribe.[53] Washington officials, however, wanted clarification. Agent Pease was requested on June 11, 1872, to determine the "wishes and desires" of the Crow in regard to relocating their agency and selling a portion of their reservation. Pease later reported the Crow were "not only willing but anxious to make a change in the location of their agency." He warned, however, that they were "suspicious, and have but little faith in the promises" made in discussions with white men.[54]

John Frost Jr. (*right*) with Plenty Coups (*center*) and White Face Bear at the White House to visit President William G. Harding. *loc.gov/item/91784482*.

With this news, government officials moved quickly, dispatching Chairman of the Board of Indian Commissioners Felix Brunot westward in the summer of 1872. Conducting business on other Indian agencies, Brunot then proceeded to Fort Parker on July 17. He had freshly concluded a treaty with the Shoshoni Indians, ceding reservation lands due to miners' prior claims, much the same scenario for his visit with the Crow.[55] Undoubtedly, he was hoping for a similar result. His expectations were quickly dashed on learning the main Crow camp of Chief Blackfoot, 140 lodges (1,400 people) were camped some 200 miles from the agency but would be there within days. A few sub-chiefs filtered in, including

Bear in the Water and Long Horse, "with ninety-six lodges [960 people]." Little else was discussed other than the tribe's preoccupation with the Sioux. The commissioner did note several important findings, for one, the "government has not made any effort" to fulfill treaty responsibilities by removing white miners and intruders from living on the reservation. Nor had they fulfilled their pledge to protect the Crow from the Sioux attacks, and "every year they meet and many of the Crow are killed." Brunot had other grievances. Among them he believed the agency location was "in no way suited" for farming practices. He also found the buildings "very poor and unsuited," the day school a "failure" and no efforts made to provide the gospel for "enlightenment" of the Crow. He considered it "useless" to expend their appropriated funds here and reckoned the place, "bad as it is," had potential to get worse. With the probable construction along the Crow's northern boundary of Northern Pacific Rail was the potential for the rails to branch to what soon would become Yellowstone National Park.[56] This would spur an ever-larger populace of intruders and greater potential for conflict on the Crow Reservation.[57]

Shortly after Brunot's visit, Fort Parker was destroyed by fire on October 30, 1872. The *Bozeman Avant Courier* reported the destruction may have been

Crow women and children (unidentified) in front of Fort Parker. *BAE GN 03422.*

caused by a former employee dumping stove ashes near the north bastion. The following night, a small fire was discovered but thought to be extinguished. By 2:00 a.m., flames driven by fierce winds had rekindled, engulfing the agency. Efforts to save the stockade and buildings were unsuccessful. The loss was significant,[58] but the calamity may have contributed to the government's impetus to settle matters with the Crow while at the same time remedy the steady influx of white settlers, miners and Sioux invasions, all before "new agency buildings are put up."[59] There was another mitigating factor that may have also weighed in for relocation of the Crow.

The issue was what to do with the River Crow, the homeless brethren band to the Mountain Crow. Brunot touched on the question during his visit to Fort Parker, gaining advice on the subject from General Bradley, formerly commander of Fort Ellis (forty miles from Fort Parker). Well acquainted with the Crow, the general was of the opinion the Mountain and River Crow should be "concentrated" on one reservation.[60]

The River Crow

On July 15, 1868, the River Crow signed an agreement at Fort Hawley, Montana, for a tract of land near the Milk River adjoining that of the Gros Ventre Tribe. Once settled, they also were to pursue an agricultural lifestyle. However, the Senate gave passage for the Fort Laramie Treaty of 1868, but the 40th Congress, in lame duck session, never ratified the River Crow treaty, thus leaving them without a reservation.[61]

Agent Fellows D. Pease described the situation early in his tenure. The Crow Indians comprise the Mountain and River Crow, "the former so called on account of hunting and roaming near the mountains away from the Missouri River" and the River Crow so called due to dwelling near the Missouri River.[62] The River Crow separated twelve years ago, he continued, "but really comprise one large family, speaking the same language, having the same customs, the same enemies and closely connected with each other through intermarriage." The agent estimated their numbers as 1,400 River Crow (and around 2,700 Mountain Crow). He noted most of the River Crow received annuities at Fort Parker and "desire" to live permanently with the Mountain Crow, although some remained with the Gros Ventres.[63] The River Crow often visited their kindred brethren at Fort Parker,[64] but attempts to lure them permanently with the Mountain Crow at Fort Parker proved unsuccessful. With that in

Mierishash (Two Belly) was a River Crow who signed the Fort Hawley Treaty. *BAE GN 03384A.*

mind, a hopeful government foresaw the opportunity to provide a new reservation where they could reunite and live and settle the score on all other affairs.[65] Government officials, including Brunot, concurred the Mountain and River Crow should be consolidated.[66]

SUMMER COUNCIL 1873

Armed with congressional approval by act of March 3, 1873, Felix Brunot returned to Fort Parker to negotiate with the Crow Tribe. "for the surrender of their reservation…or of such part thereof as may be consistent with the welfare of said Indians."[67] However, the era of treaty making had been abolished by an appropriation act of March 3, 1871. The fine print was in a bill with Yankton Sioux Indians, stating, "No Indian nation or tribe within the territory of the United States shall be acknowledged or recognized as an independent nation, tribe, or power." Instead, the act called for formal agreements be made rather than treaties. Ratification from both houses of Congress would be required, rather than just Senate approval.[68]

Brunot was accompanied from Washington by General Eliphalet Whittlesey and Thomas Cree, as secretary. Dr. James Wright, superintendent of Indian affairs for Montana, would also be present. The commission hoped to meet with both the main body of tribe, the Mountain Crow, numbering about 3,200 strong, and the River Crow, totaling around 1,200.[69] The commissioners reached Fort Parker on July 31, 1873, to find most of the tribal leaders had not yet arrived.

The next day, Chief Blackfoot and a few principal men called on the commissioners, "singing" a welcome song. An impatient Brunot wanted to "see all the Crows" but was told the Mountain Crow had been delayed after an encounter with the Lakota Sioux near the mouth of Pryor Creek. The River Crow were detained near the Missouri River by traders who were fearful they would lose their business if they relocated.[70] "Do not be in a hurry," cautioned Blackfoot, battle weary and mourning the loss of his brother. Our people "want to see you," he assured the commissioner, but the Crow camp was several days away, the horses in "poor" condition and the swollen streams "hard to cross."

To the impatient commission's annoyance, proceedings were not held until August 11. Brunot wasted no time explaining to those assembled the Crow Reservation boundaries were no longer practicable due to the increase in miners, settlements and potential for trouble. He warned in all probability the Northern Pacific Railroad would be built along the Yellowstone River, disturbing prime game habitat, thus making a successful hunt difficult. He suggested the Crow sell the mountainous area and a "better" agency location would be built.

Prior to Blackfoot's response to the officials, he lit a pipe, stating just as they speak with Jesus, the Crow way to communicate was through E-so-we-wat-se, the "Great Spirit." The great leader pleaded for the "white man and the Indian speak the truth to each other today" and then passed the pipe to the commissioners as an oath for them to do the same. When he was done talking, several Crow came forward with gifts of buffalo robes and two horses for the commissioners, who declined them. "When the Crows meet a friend, they always give them something; so we do with you," explained Blackfoot, and "you ought to take it."

Blackfoot moved into a lengthy oratory, explaining, "The Great Spirit made these mountains and rivers for us, and all this land." He reminded the council of the Crows' long-standing friendship with the whites and chided the government for supplying the Sioux weapons and also for their failures to keep miners from "stealing our quartz." "Look at me," he pleaded. "I am a big man. I have a big heart, and what I say is true. The whites have been digging gold at Emigrant Gulch for ten years. Perhaps the white men think the Crows do not know it, but we do know all about it," he added. An apologetic Brunot explained the miners were located on the land before the treaty was signed.

Pulling out a map, the commissioner pointed to a proposed reservation for them in the Judith Basin region and of its advantages. He warned this area between the Missouri and Musselshell Rivers might become occupied if they waited too long and suggested they exchange it for their present reservation. The council was then interrupted by Crow weeping and singing mourning songs due to their losses in the recent battle.

When the council resumed, Blackfoot announced the Crow Tribe would remain on their present reservation, but they were willing to sell the area occupied by the miners and a belt of land to route the new railroad. This did not please Brunot. It "would do no good," he stated, to sell only a small portion. He rationalized white men would continue to encroach and the "same trouble" would start all over. It was much like selling a good horse or moving to a different place; a man does not like to make a change but knows what is best and "thinks of it." He suggested they consider it before "our words are lost" and it was "too late."

Due to rain on the fourth day, no general council was held, although the chiefs "gathered" and discussed the proposal all afternoon. On the fifth day, Blackfoot countered the area was occupied by "trappers and hunters…poisoning game…Sioux Indians, Cree, Santees, Mandans, Assineboines [sic], Gros Ventres" and many tribes and white men. He concluded, "We will likely quarrel. That is what we think about." In regard to the proposed size of the Judith Basin reservation, represented as area 557, the younger men agreed to Brunot's draft while the wizened chiefs,

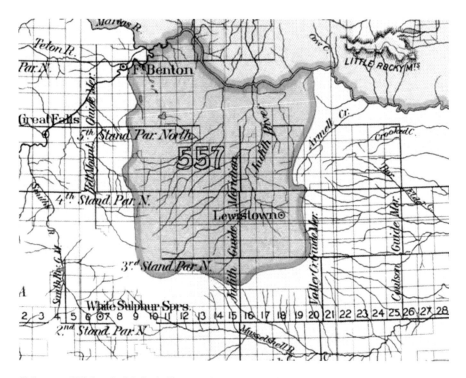

"Montana 2" Map, Judith Basin Reserve. *https://memory.loc.gov/ammem/amlaw/lwss-ilc.html.*

Iron Bull and Blackfoot, argued for a more vast expanse. "You want to give us a little hole," the latter stated. "We want a big country; you gave the Sioux a big country, and the Crows are a big tribe and want a big country." Old Crow claimed, "If we take Judith Basin we can shoot from one line of our country to the other line."

An impatient Brunot told them a decision was needed. They had three choices: (1) exchange their reservation and receive a payment for the difference in value, (2) sell a portion of their present reservation or (3) do nothing at all. Blackfoot negotiated for an enlarged Judith Basin reservation. Even though it was unusual to do so, speaking in agreement was a Crow woman, "The one who goes straight along." She also did not want the "little country."

However, Brunot urged Crow members to come forward and sign the pact. If not, he would return to Washington, D.C. The commissioner persuaded all the leading chiefs but Blackfoot to consent, but the sixth and final day found every leading chief signing the agreement on August 16, 1873.[71]

The Earl of Dunraven, a British adventurer visiting the Crow at Fort Parker in 1874, wrote about the negotiations in his book *The Great Divide*. Based on his exchange with the Crow, he concluded they had no choice but to sign.[72] The scene below, *Counting his coups*, was taken from his book. The Crow, in fact, were weary from battling with the Sioux near Pryor Creek. Some, such as Long Horse, who lost a brother, were in mourning, and others were sick. Both Iron Bull and Blackfoot were affected with erysipelas, a skin disease, Iron Bull even withdrawing during a portion of the meeting.[73]

"The Crow Indians Talked Out of Their Reservation, The Crow Indians Plucked," boldly headlined the *New York Herald*, clearly expressing eastern sentiments. This was in sharp contrast to Montana governor Benjamin Potts's excitement over the "great patience" Brunot demonstrated in concluding the agreement. Reducing the reservation for one about a third of the size was a "wise and humane" choice for both Indians and "every good citizen in Montana." Potts predicted the ceded area, "one of the finest and most extensive valleys on the continent," would rapidly be filled with the Northern Pacific Railroad and increasing settlements.[74]

Counting his coups. From The Earl of Dunraven, The Great Divide: Travels in the Upper Yellowstone in the Summer of 1874.

FORT SHERMAN

One thing was left to complete the new home for the Crow, a selection of a suitable agency site within the confines of the new reservation. It quickly became a competitive affair. Businessmen Nelson Story and Charles W. Hoffman, both conspicuously present during the Judith Basin negotiations, were eager for an opportunity to turn a profit from trade. Also contending was Fellows Pease, who in cooperation with Lieutenant Gustavus Doane, a military officer from Fort Ellis, anticipated the two of them would select a site.[75] Doane, familiar with the Judith Basin, had previously discussed the ideal location with Commissioner Brunot,[76] while the Indian Bureau had other plans for Pease. Even though Pease had been discharged from his position as Crow agent, he was selected to travel as a special agent with a delegation of Crow to Washington.[77] In his absence, newly appointed Crow agent James Wright swiftly hired agency employees, Robert Cross, farmer, and Horace Countryman, "a practical miller and engineer," to find "a suitable site." Among the prerequisites was the need for adequate waterpower to propel a sawmill and wheat mill, ample timber and fertile farm ground. Mitch Boyer, "well acquainted with all the intervening country," was hired to guide them.[78] The Cross/Countryman party not only selected a site, but it was the very one Doane had previously suggested as well.[79] It was then arranged for traders Nelson Story and Charles W. Hoffman to establish a post nearby.[80] This pair swiftly hired Peter Koch, former wood-hawk, Fort Ellis clerk and businessman, for one hundred dollars a month. He soon had wagons bound for the site.[81] This invasion in the heart of Crow hunting grounds was not taken lightly by Chief Blackfoot, who did not "want anybody to go in there without his knowledge."[82]

CROW DELEGATION TO WASHINGTON

The Crow were familiar with stories of Red Cloud and the Sioux delegation traveling to Washington and anxious to talk in person with their Great Father, believing this way promises would be more faithfully kept.[83] Felix Brunot arranged for a delegation of Crow leaders to journey to Washington D.C. The ploy to invite important tribal members to the nation's capital to meet with the president, secretary of war, commissioner of Indian affairs and other dignitaries was believed beneficial. For most Native Americans, the only contact with white men was in the form of fighting, killing or escaping during a battle.[84]

Delegation travel to Washington was also used to convince tribes of the futility of war, impressing not only the benevolent hand of the government but also its power and might. In short, nothing was spared "in the effort to deepen the impressions" on visiting Indian delegations.[85] Although no longer their agent, Fellows Pease was commissioned to travel with the Crow delegation.[86]

The Crow were not pleased to hear Fellows Pease would be not be retained as Crow agent. He "never treated us wrong," remarked Blackfoot to commissioners visiting in 1873. "We do not want Pease to go away," echoed Crazy Sister in Law, whose son offered government officials a horse for his retention. At the same time, gifts of buffalo robes were presented to Pease by daughters of Crazy Sister in Law and Mountain Chief. "We want Pease to stay with the Crow Tribe," they pleaded. In fact, it was reported, "All the children gathered about Major Pease to hold on to him."[87] This high regard the Crow held for Pease may have influenced the government decision to obtain his services as escort for the Crow to Washington. Ever since one tribal member journeyed to Washington and subsequently did not return, the Crow were found "unwilling" to do so. Their confidence in their former agent would offer a measure of comfort.

The October 5, 1873 issue of the *Helena Weekly Herald* printed notice of the Crow delegation departure from Fort Parker. "We doubt a finer body of Indians ever visited the Great Father before. They are fine looking, remarkably intelligent, and have always been true friends of the whites."[88] The delegation's great journey to the East began via stagecoach from Virginia City, Montana, to Corrine, Utah.[89] From Utah they traveled by rail to Council Bluffs, Iowa, then to Chicago. The *Chicago Daily Tribune* observed the Crow were "amused" by a visit to the Hooley's Theatre, a circus performance and the Academy of Music, certainly all an eyeful for the travelers. In return, the Crow "gave a grand exhibition of war dances and songs in the dining room of the Sherman" hotel, no doubt equally thrilling and foreign to Chicago's elite.[90] Travel rigors and an unaccustomed immunity triggered illness among several delegates, requiring medicine.[91] Nonetheless they departed Chicago on October 15 for their Great Father's home in Washington.[92]

Accounts of the Crow council on October 21 with Commissioner of Indian Affairs Edward P. Smith and their old acquaintance Felix Brunot became headline news in Washington's *Evening Star.* "The chiefs were gorgeous in their red paint, feather, horse-hair fringes, and beads, and each one carried a fan or long brush, (resembling a duster,) made of light brown feathers. All of them wore ponderous brass ear-rings…[and] red or blue blankets or buffalo skins." Their attire proven to withstand vigorous cold western weather proved to be too warm for inside speaking engagements, prompting Blackfoot to remark "it is pretty warm in here," spawning "laughter" from the audience and some confusion for the Crow.

Before moving into any further discussion, Iron Bull filled his "long calumet" pipe. Considered a vow to pledge the truth, the pipe was then passed to Brunot and other dignitaries, "each of whom took a pull at it" while the Crow delegation waited in a "a dignified silence." Then in a room "blue with smoke, Blackfoot arose and shook hands with Mr. Brunot and others, looking each person straight in the face for a few seconds." The guest then spoke of the tribe's loyalty and friendship to the white men. "All the tribes of the plains that come to see the Father have bloody hands. I have not, I want to be friendly."[93] Blackfoot spoke of troubles with the Sioux, acknowledging they fought four times over the course of the summer. "We fight for the land," he clarified. Even so, Blackfoot reminded the council, the Crow were amenable to the government and said "yes" to the sale of

Interior of Hooley's Theatre. *digital.library.illinois.edu/items/ef0d2890-1a05-0134-1d6d-0050569601ca-4.*

their sacred "medicine land…mountains, and the hills."[94] He admitted they sold their country in return for one with grim prosects, "a country in which there is no wood, no water, and no grass; nothing but rocks," and requested government leaders "take pity" and agree to additional land for his people in the Judith Basin.[95] His comments seemingly had no effect.

The 1873 Crow delegation was photographed in a Washington, D.C. studio. *Sitting, left to right*: Stays with the Horses (Bear Wolf's wife) and Good Medicine Pipe (Old Crow's wife); *middle*: Bear Wolf (Se-ta-pit-se), White Calf (Te-shu-nzt), Chief Blackfoot (Kam-ne-but-se), Iron Bull (Che-ve-te Pu-ma-ta), One Who Lead the Old Dog (Pish-ki-ha-di-ri-ky-ish) and Chief Old Crow (Perits-har-sts); *back*: Long Horse (Eche-has-ka), Thin Belly (Ella-causs-se), Bernard Prero (Bravo, interpreter), Blackfoot's wife, Agent Pease, Iron Bull's wife, Pierre Chien (interpreter) and Mo-mukh-pi-tche.

A second news account describes the tribe's long-anticipated meeting on October 24 with President Ulysses S. Grant. Deploying a similar tactic, Blackfoot, speaking on behalf of the Crow, reminded the president "his tribe had always been friendly with the whites," adding the remains of the Crow and soldiers lie together, "fallen in warfare against the Sioux."

The 1873 Crow Delegation. *NAA INV 10000238; OPPS NEG 3431 B.*

Grant acknowledged their friendship and hoped they would continue that state of "mind." Then he "counseled" the necessity for the Crow to farm and ready themselves in the future without government "care" and aide.

The president took the delegation to meet Julia Grant and their daughter, then were whisked off to a naval yard and given a Gatling gun demonstration as proof of the government's power. Impressed with its lethalness, the wife of Blackfoot queried, "Why do you not bring such guns against the Sioux?"[96]

In a second council on October 29 with Commissioner Smith, the Crow reiterated their concerns, most notably for the inclusion of the Musselshell country in the recent agreement. Thin Belly noted, "The Great Father put me right in the middle of all the enemies of the prairies." White Calf remarked, "I came a great distance to see my Great Father" and then suggested the "white men to go back with us to the Muscle Shell and eat buffalo with us."[97] The Crow also noted concerns to retain Pease as their agent. "He treats me and my children good. I like him," stated Long Horse.

Third was the delegation's preoccupation with settling the score with the Sioux. Old Dog suggested the government allow him to "do something" about their old foe. Smith acknowledged their concerns and reminded the delegation the treaty was already signed and if they altered it now the payment amount might also change. Smith then explained their desire to retain Pease "cannot be settled" as the Crow wished. Before the council dispersed, the Crow requested spending money to purchase gifts, something no other delegation had done or been given. The bargainers asked for a $100 but settled for $50.[98]

The delegation faced their homeward journey with a stop in New York. The *New York Herald* reported their arrival and stay November 3 at the Grand Central Hotel, commenting the Crow "would prove a very attractive show for the curiosity seekers."[99] For the Crow, this lengthy eight-day stay provided ample opportunity for sightseeing but found many of the Crow, previously sick, had worsened. Both Blackfoot and Thin Belly became "very ill" with an "attack of lung fever."[100] A layover was required, with the hotel providing amenities, including meals in rooms, baths, cigars and, for those willing, carriage rides and boat trip to Long Island. The weary and homesick[101] Crow finally departed New York on November 7, bound for Philadelphia.[102] Rather than face the "crowded" conditions they experienced in the stagecoach and unfamiliar food,[103] the Crow were set on purchasing horses to ride from Corrine, Utah, back to Fort Parker. However, due to the extreme cold weather, they declined[104] and instead boarded the stagecoach northbound for Virginia City.

Above: Eche-Has-Ka (Long Horse), Kam-Ne-Butse (Blackfoot) and Te-Shu-Nzt (White Calf). *BAE GN 03420*.

Opposite: Mo-Mukh-Pi-Tche, Ella-Causs-Se (Thin Belly) and Pish-Ki-Ha-Di-Ri-Ky-Ish (One Who Leads The Old Dog). *BAE GN 03419*.

On the heels of their arrival in Virginia City, the territorial capital of Montana, Blackfoot sought out Governor Benjamin Potts. The chief requested the governor send his plea to President Grant, again urging for the addition of the Musselshell country in the new Crow treaty.[105] "It will make our hearts the most glad of anything you can do for us," implored the chief.[106]

The Crow returned to Fort Parker in early December 1873. During their absence, Montana citizens, gripped by the fact the Judith Basin was to be set aside as a reservation for the Crow, developed a keen interest in the area.

A HOPE CALLED CARROLL

In the early 1870s, the small settlement of log cabins called Carroll had hopes of replacing Fort Benton as Montana Territory's steamboat navigation and shipping center on the Missouri River. Fort Benton, upstream, was often unreliable due to seasonal shallow water and a long set of rapids. Carroll, on the other hand, was farther downriver, providing a saving on shipping costs, while it also had a prolonged season due to greater water flow. Promoters sought to build a wagon road from Carroll across the Judith Basin to Helena.[107] Weighing in was the financial panic of 1873, which halted construction on the Northern Pacific Railroad near Bismarck, Dakota Territory. The railroad, not wanting to lose trade, made an agreement with the Diamond R Freight Company. The railroad proposed bringing the goods to Bismarck, then loading them on steamboats bound for Carroll, and from there freighted by the Diamond R to Helena.

Carroll, pictured in 1881. *H-00341 Haynes Coll. MHS.*

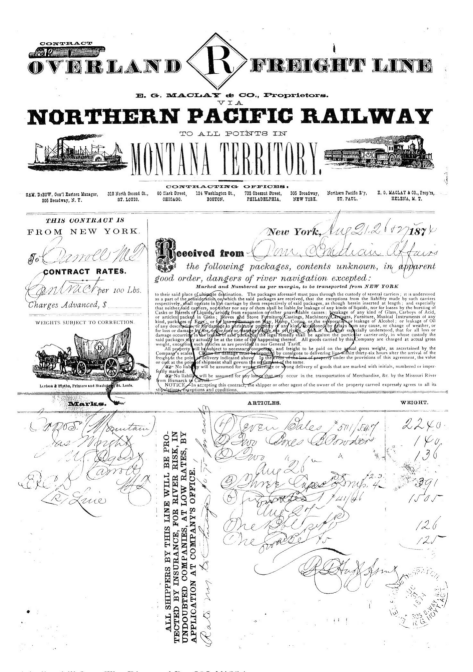

A lading bill from The Diamond R. *r505-NA234.*

In 1873, the Diamond R, recognizing the new Crow Reservation would end this project, actively cut a trail to Carroll. The following year, the company convinced the U.S. Army to establish a series of posts along the trail to protect it from Indian raids. Soon, the Carroll Trail was promoted as the most reliable route for getting supplies to and from the new capital of Helena, Montana Territory.[108]

When the document creating the new Judith Basin Reservation was submitted to Congress on January 17, 1874, and the affected lands withdrawn from the public, powerful civilian interests, including proponents of the Carroll Road, trading posts and cattlemen, pressured politicians. These protestors were more than happy to abolish the old Crow Reservation but not in favor of the creation of the new one, even if it were one-third in size to its predecessor. Congress delayed any actions, and the lack of treaty ratification brought discontent among the Crow. Despite the leading chiefs' signatures, the Indian Office did not press for bill approval and the agreement was never ratified by Congress. The lands returned to public domain on March 27, 1874. The Judith Basin reserve became a dead issue,[109] and the Crow remained at Fort Parker. The unratified agreement in the Judith Basin did not, however, end the issue of relocating the Crow. This would become the crusade of Dr. James Wright.

James Wright

James Wright, a native of Indiana, was born in 1817. He moved to Delaware County, Iowa, around 1852. Two years later, he was elected clerk of the court, holding office until 1862, when he was elected secretary of state. To this office he was reelected in 1864. By 1872, he had been appointed Montana superintendent of Indian affairs, posting bond on Christmas Day.[110] Dr. Wright, ordained as a Methodist Episcopal minister, was touchy about temperance, and his views on the suppression of liquor traffic were expressed to the secretary of the interior even before leaving Iowa to assume his new job in Montana.[111]

He also emphasized the need for Montana agencies to set an example by employing "reliable Christian men…of moral standing of strict and tempered habits."[112] The superintendent's first visit to Fort Parker on March 4, 1873, quickly darkened after discovering "several employees living with Indian women out of lawful wedlock." He immediately ordered Agent Pease to notify the parties to legally marry within thirty days or be removed from the reservation, thus losing their jobs.[113]

CROW NUPTIALS

Within a month, a Methodist minister, Reverend Matthew Bird, arrived at Fort Parker to officiate marriages between Crows and whites.[114] One employee, William Parker, was discharged for refusing to marry his girlfriend Mary.[115] Parker did later wed Mary, also called Bad Woman.

Several more couples complied with the order including a woman also called Mary, or Sees Plain, and Barney Bravo or Prevo. Bravo was an agency messenger and interpreter who traveled to Washington, D.C., with the Crow delegation in 1873. Mitch Bouyer also wed a Crow bride by the name of Mary. Mitch was later killed in the Battle of the Little Big Horn. Tom Leforge was another agency employee who married a Crow woman. His account and details were recorded by his biographer, Thomas B. Marquis, in *Memoirs of a White Crow Indian*. Leforge's wife-to-be was

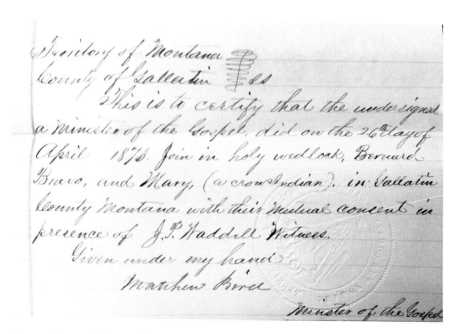

Barney Bravo wedding certificate. *"Certificates of Marriage, 1856–1888," Gallatin County Clerk and Recorder Office, Bozeman, Montana.*

Mary Parker. *035 B03f01.01 Bud Lake Coll. MHS.*

Cherry, a tall and attractive Crow girl, [who] became to me unusually interesting. She had brown hair, hazel eyes, evidently was of mixed race, although I never did learn the source of her white blood. I conceived a special liking—or perhaps it was a deliberate cultivation of liking-for her brother whose name was Head-and-Tail Robe. I visited often with him at their tepee lodge. During these visits I never spoke directly to the girl. Yet, by means of the mysterious telepathy that flashes between congenial spirits, I came to know that she preferred me above all other young men.[116]

Tom Leforge (*seated, left, with hat*). Possibly adjacent is Cherry, whom he married. *Calfee-Catlin ST 002.095 MHS.*

Leforge "obeyed" Wright's order demanding white men living with Indian women be married "in due" form, which he and others did. His wedding was consummated by the "ring ceremony." Cherry, his wife, "wore hers as long as she lived." Barney Bravo interpreted at the marriage, while Leforge did the same for Bravo.[117]

Thomas Kent and Elisabeth, called What She Has Is Well Known, also took vows. It has been stated her husband paid five head of fine horses, guns, ammunition, blankets and more for her.[118] Kent was an employee at Fort Parker and later the Absaroka Agency, where he sold beef.

Another cross-cultural wedding was Tom Shane and eighteen-year-old Strikes the Gun, a River Crow. Her father, Four Times, was a band leader and her mother was called Medicine Cherry Tree.[119] Strikes the Gun took the married name of Sarah Shane.

Even with the flush of weddings, Superintendent Wright was still not content with the moral fiber of those at the agency. He loathed idleness and the collection of white men who "lounged around the agency and Indian Camps subsisting the best they could" from rations provided to employed white men or food supplied by the Crow. "Of this the Indians bitterly complain," he alleged.[120]

Tom Leforge acknowledged the ease of this lifestyle: "any white man could live among the Crow without need for toil." Annuities and rations doled out to the Crow women through treaty claims enabled wives to be the "breadwinner."[121] Leforge did concede some of the men married to Crow women "were ambitious, were good workers, and a few of them prospered. But others were absolute vagabonds." They were termed "squaw-man," but over time, explained Leforge, the phrase was used to describe any white man married to an Indian.[122]

Instead of solving issues with matrimonial bliss, Wright created a deeper rift. He next questioned the legitimacy of any unemployed white man's presence on the reservation. Can they "stay as long as they please," he queried or be "forcibly" be removed?[123] Of those married, Wright continued to fault their character and habits, most notably those regularly inebriated, believing they were "detrimental" and "demoralizing" to the Crow.[124] Wright may have been offended, but Blackfoot recalled the white men who came to live near Sheep Mountain (located across the Yellowstone River from Fort Parker) "are my friends; they marry Crow women, they have children…and talk Crow.…We get off at their doors and they give us food. We like it." He added Pierre Chien, the Crow interpreter, was just a boy when he came to live with the Crow. "We raised" him, elaborated the chief.[125]

Mary Kent. *Wilcox/Kemph Collection, Museum of the Beartooths (MOB)*.

Standing: Katie (Mrs. Jim Burton), Tom Doyle (in doorway), Maggie (Mrs. Tom Doyle), Pat and Jirah Allen; *seated*: Tom Shane, Bessie, Sarah Shane and Josie. *MOB.*

Wright found a surprising outcome of the mixed marriages due to the fact many of the Crow wives appeared eager to take advantage of promised farming provisions under Article VI and VIII of the 1868 treaty . Within months of their matrimony, he submitted to his superiors a sizeable list of those who wished to farm—the first group effort nearly six years after the signing of the treaty. It was hoped they would set an example as encouragement for others to farm.[126]

Wright, however, was more of a proponent of raising livestock than farming, observing accurately that the Crow Reservation is "fine stock country…and The Crow Indians have a passion for stock. They delight in horses, and say

A partial list of Crow beginning to farm. *Oct. 30, 1874, r.500-NA234.*

they would love to have herds of cattle." He reasoned beef rations were raised by white cattlemen for Crow consumption on reservation grass. The Crow "have as good [a] right to this grass," and raising cattle would not require much effort. "One man with a few Indian boys could handle a large number of cattle," he added,[127] then proposed the government purchase $50,000 of "young" stock for beef consumption and also to perpetuate a breeding herd.[128] However, knowing it was the government's unwavering goal for the Indian become self-sufficient as farmers, Wright felt as long as the buffalo were abundant, they had no reason to do so. The pragmatist rationalized it would take a two-step process. "First herding then tilling the soil. As soon as the buffalo is gone, they will have to resort to some other means or die. Time alone can tell which they will chose," he added harshly.[129]

BENSONS LANDING

A troublesome snare vexing Agent Wright was the small burg known as Bensons Landing. It would become an additional arsenal for the agent's insistence to relocate the Crow agency.[130] At issue here was a clause about whiskey blanketed under the Intercourse Law. The law, first formulated in 1790, with subsequent amendments, existed namely to state what may and may not be been done in Indian Country. Trade with Indians was prohibited in Indian Country without a license; penalties were also set for anyone caught illegally selling or trading liquor to them.

What constituted "Indian Country" became a bone of contention between Indian affairs commissioners and the traders. Traders claimed that if they were not on the actual reservation, they were not subject to the laws. In an attempt to curb whiskey trade, legal authorities declared "Indian Country" as all areas where men approached reservations and places inhabited or frequented by Indians.[131] Quick to outwit, traders lined themselves along riversides opposite reservation boundaries, such as Bensons Landing, to conduct their business.

Bensons was located nine miles west of Fort Parker on the north bank of the Yellowstone River, therefore off the Crow Reservation. By 1873, Amos Benson and Dan Naileigh had opened a saloon here.[132] Hugo J. Hoppy and his wife, Mary Jane, were also proprietors of a nearby trading post. It was said Mary Jane became quite skilled as a trader, gaining a reputation among the Crow as an honest and caring sort.[133]

The small cluster of log cabins became a well-known point on the Yellowstone, and depending on what side of the fence you were on, it was either an indulgence or "serious nuisance."[134] For temperate-minded Wright, it was the latter.[135]

Lashing out to the commissioner of Indian Affairs, he explained Bensons was a "rendezvous for all the bummers and followers of Indian Camps, and illicit traders." Unrestricted trade was perceived legitimate here, and Wright did his best to restrain the Crow from going. However, he understood they were "enticed" by runners sent into their camps.[136] He quickly discerned Bensons held an added attraction for the Crow and other tribes, namely, the means to trade for some of their most coveted items—ammunition and arms. At Bensons, the "unlicensed traders, and irresponsible men...sold them all the cartridges they wanted" reported Wright."[137] This was converse to the licensed traders whose hands were tied. Fearing weapons and ammunition would fall into the hands of hostile Indians, they were forbidden at this time by the secretary of the interior to offer trades.[138] Wright warned if the illicit trading shops were allowed to continue, "then farewell to good order and peace amongst these people."[139]

Shades of conflict had already darkened Bensons; one volatile incident was recalled by Tom Leforge. He explained that occasionally dances and feasts were held at the settlement to attract Indian trade. One evening, Leforge and his bride traveled there for supper and a dance. The event turned lively when "a bullet crashed through the [window] glass and hit the opposite wall." The diners quickly dove for shelter and then later made a thorough search, firing "random" shots in the darkness, but no guilty party was found.[140]

Equally unpredictable and potentially as charged were the horse races waged "nearly every day" at the outpost. The competition between settlers and Native populations "as a general thing" realized a loss to the "white's side."[141] The Crow prided themselves with owning superior horses, as a fast horse was invaluable for hunting needs but also added allure to an individual warrior's presence.[142]

HUNTERS HOT SPRINGS

Hunters Hot Springs is another example of the turmoil and lawlessness commonplace near Fort Parker. Hunters in particular became a hotbed for Sioux and Piegan (a band of the Blackfoot Indian Nation) depredations. Dr. Hunter's daughter, Lizzie Hunter Rich, recalled the surrounding country often would be "overrun by renegade war parties' intent on killing." Frequently, the children were securely locked in their cabin, one time stuffed up the chimney, while their mother stood guard on an elevated hill to warn those working the field. Troubles with raiding parties frequently emerged when the Crows were absent, down the river or away on their buffalo hunts. "The Crows were a great protection to us," she claimed, and were regularly camped nearby. The spring and summer of 1873 were especially troublesome for the Hunters. Often, near Fort Parker, they witnessed Sioux Indians who had signal fires burning at night. During the daylight, flashes from mirrors atop nearby mountains were used as signs. In 1874, a party of Sioux jumped Dr. Hunter at his ranch. After exchanging gunfire, eleven Sioux escaped, mounted on Hunter's "fine" horses. A military force from Fort Ellis gave pursuit, eventually scattering the Sioux into the hills. During the action, a ranch hand was found dead with six arrows in him.[143] During another alarm, Iron Bull stopped at the Hunters' residence, insisting they accompany him for a buffalo hunt. After several days without any game, the Crow leader told the Hunter family they could return home. Hunter was

Che-Ve-Te-Pu-Ma-Ta (Iron Bull) and with his wife in 1873. *BAE GN 03379.*

perplexed but soon learned the Piegan Indians had again invaded the valley. Iron Bull had lured them away from potential danger.[144]

Relocation Woes

Due to "remote" timber sources, inadequate farm ground and "very uncomfortable" winds, Superintendent Wright was never in favor of the agency location at Fort Parker and advocated for its relocation.[145] He continued the cause when his title as superintendent was abolished and he assumed duties as Crow agent on September 20, 1873.[146] He began his relocation crusade in earnest after Congress's failure to ratify the 1873 agreement for retention of the Judith Basin for the Crow. Wright declared the very appeal of the basin to serve the Crow, "its isolated position—has been destroyed." He believed the fact the railroad would "pass" nearby the present reservation was no reason for "disposing" of the land. To the "contrary," Crow country would become more "valuable," especially when they began farming. However, due to the fact the present reservation border and Fort Parker were close to the river, lending opportunity for "unprincipled white men" to smuggle in whiskey, Agent Wright pressed Commissioner of Indian Affairs Edward P. Smith to relocate the Crow to a more suitable and isolated agency location.[147] Wright also noted Fort Parker was "hard to defend" from hostile Indians. "Besides," he added, it did not "suit" the Crow. On this the Crow agreed. "This is not the place for the agency, on this point of rocks," Blackfoot once remarked. "We would like to know who built the agency here."[148]

Wright advised "good locations from forty to sixty miles east" of the agency could be found and recommended moving the agency as quickly as "practicable."[149] In October 1874, he was ordered by government officials to find a new agency site. However, his request to be transferred to another Indian agency turned over the duty to his replacement, Dexter E. Clapp.[150]

3

AGENT DEXTER CLAPP
AND THE ABSAROKA AGENCY

D exter Elisha Clapp was born in Genesee County, New York, June 7, 1830. In 1854, Clapp graduated from Genesee College, receiving a master of fine arts degree and the same degree from the University of New York. After leaving college, he entered the Methodist Episcopal Church. In 1862, he entered the army as captain of Company C, 148th New York State Volunteers. For most of the Civil War, he commanded the 38th Regiment, Colored Infantry. During the winter of 1864, he was in command of the 1st Brigade of the 3rd Division of the 18th Army Corps.

Clapp was active in many battles and various campaigns around Richmond and brevetted brigadier general of volunteers for gallant conduct. After the war, he served as minister to the Argentine Confederation in South America. Resigning this position, he went to Kansas, settling on a tract of raw prairie land. Subsequently he was appointed Crow agent in Montana Territory at Fort Parker. A local paper noted that Clapp and his wife arrived in Bozeman on November 30, 1874. The following day, they proceeded to Fort Parker.[151] Clapp assumed official duties on December 7. He served for nearly two years.[152]

First Duties

Agent Clapp's first pressing duty was to find a suitable location for a new Crow agency within the confines of their reservation, preferably one farther removed from invading gold miners and dubious traders. He departed

Fort Parker on December 16, 1874, with Lieutenant Gustavus Doane and other soldiers dispatched from Fort Ellis, a military post near Bozeman, Montana. Six days later, he reported, "I found only two good locations for an Agency, one at the mouth of Deer Creek on the Yellowstone, and one at the junction of the Stillwater and Rosebud Creeks. There are good supplies of timber and water, and sufficient—excellent—tillable land at each of these places." He recommended relocating the agency to the Rosebud site, for it was deeper within the reservation, offering a secure barrier from "whiskey selling and other illicit trading" and better potential for peace. Second, he noted the site provided "opportunity for farming operations…[and] for raising supplies, practically impossible at the present location." Lastly, "the Stillwater Valley is out of the line of the terrible Yellowstone canon [*sic*] winds" and "comparatively free from certain 'rheumatic diseases.'"[153]

Clapp Encounters Stumbling Blocks

While Clapp was engaged in formulating plans for the new agency, the traders at Bensons Landing began tactics of their own. Not only had they increased in numbers, but, fearing their livelihood in jeopardy, also "raised a storm of excitement" to incite the Crow into a "violent opposition" over relocating.[154]

The traders were abetted by local newspaper claims the Crow were "divided" about moving their new agency, noting it would be located near their favorite hunting ground, thus spooking away wild game.[155] The military at Fort Ellis, displeased the new agency would be farther away from their post and therefore more difficult and dangerous to protect, dispatched Captain George Tyler to discern their "feelings."[156] The officer reported the Crow "are very much dissatisfied," not only due to scaring away game but also because the change would "attract white men into their favorite hunting country." They voiced concerns that the deep snowfall would make it difficult for their ponies to "subsist." Tyler also found opposition on account of leaving behind their dead buried at Fort Parker.[157] To his credit, Clapp acknowledged their apprehensiveness was "partly genuine" but quickly snapped most of it was "stirred up and fostered" by the Benson whiskey traders. The agent assured Commissioner of Indian Affairs Edward. P. Smith that he discussed the relocation "carefully, and repeatedly with the principal chiefs" and soothed their fears.[158] The astute and high-ranking military official Colonel John Gibbon agreed, surmising Crow discontent was more than likely influenced by traders not wishing to lose their profits.[159]

FEARS OF A SIOUX/CROW ALLIANCE

Local Bozeman residents from Gallatin Valley also chimed in to muddle the waters. Businessman John V. Bogert, realizing his own potential trade loss, alleged he had personal knowledge the Crow were dissatisfied over the agency removal, quipping he was "positively advised some of the influential chiefs declare they will never visit it upon any account." More foreboding was Bogert's declaration the Crow were contemplating taking up sides "with the Sioux against the whites."[160] This apprehension was shared by Fort Ellis's Captain D.W. Benham, who, contrary to Clapp's assurances, found the Crow "in a very disturbed condition" and "bitterly opposed to the removal of their Agency." Benham warned it was best not "to destroy the good feeling which [has] existed between the Crow Indians and the whites."[161] Clapp reflected this thread was sensationalized by the local papers "constantly announcing" the Crow were so opposed to relocating "they would join the Sioux in hostilities."[162] One *Avant Courier* reporter sensed an "apprehensive atmosphere" and exclaimed "a large faction in the Crow camps have been anxious to join the Sioux for some time." He believed bands of Long Horse, Old Crow and others were "restrained only by the influence of the older and wiser men" and warned the slightest provocation would tip the "scale in favor of the Sioux and the war-path."[163]

Rumors and fears the Crow would ally with their longtime Sioux enemy surfaced and were dispelled time and time again. "The Sioux and the Crows are at war," Chief Blackfoot evenly stated in 1873. "They offered [in 1868] to give us two hundred and sixty horses and mules, all taken from the white men, if we would join them; but we refused to do so. But I pulled loose from them and would not do so....I gave my right hand to the whites, and would hold on to them."[164]

However, more recent allegations circling in military quarters claimed Chief Bull Goes Hunting with

Born circa 1815–20, Bull Goes Hunting was a noted leader. *ST 004.05 MHS.*

forty-five to fifty lodges were willing to make peace with the Sioux.[165] This great warrior was on eleven successful war parties and rescued six men wounded in battle.[166] It is likely his words were misconstrued, but even so the threat of his potential allegiance with the Sioux would gain them a fierce warrior and cause alarm in military circles. Other Crow tribal members continued to pledge loyalty to the whites; Blackfoot "considered himself as a Whiteman in his friendship," while Little Iron and Long Horse were said to be found praying "to the Great Spirit to witness that their hearts were" with the whites.[167]

Despite Crow pledges of reliance, the government took a cautious approach and kept an eye on them, literally and figuratively. An example is found in an earlier census, listing a tally of 650 to 750 fighting-age Crow, owning 833 breechloading guns. This verified that if the Crow allied with another tribe, they would be a significant force to reckon with. To keep abreast of Crow whereabouts and plans, military scouts were dispatched periodically to their camps, hoping to garner insight on not only their state of mind but also future camp and hunting destinations.[168]

Savvy Fort Ellis post commander Major Nathanial B. Sweitzer had a different twist on the situation. He calculated it would be a lucrative business for the Crow to partner with the Sioux. Knowing the Sioux were "rich in horses," the Crow could exchange arms and ammo for a "profitable trade." As a precaution, Sweitzer reminded the Crow they were allowed to trade for guns and ammunition for hunting and defensive purposes only. He warned them also to "keep away" from the Sioux "and not make any peace without the knowledge and consent of the Government" or trading privileges for arms will be "taken away."[169] In reality, the Sioux/Crow rivalry was so "intense" the government had little cause to fear an alliance.[170]

Most certainly these undercurrents and conflicting news about potential agency relocation and temperament of the Crow caused uneasiness for Agent Clapp. Anxiously awaiting and then pressing the commissioner of Indian affairs to take "preliminary steps" for final approval, Clapp suggested that if the appropriated money was not authorized, other coffers should be considered. He offered a willingness to sacrifice amenities, believing it is "better [to] put up with many inconveniences than to remain here."[171] His pleas did not go unheard. Final approval was given by Commissioner of Indian Affairs Edward P. Smith on March 22, 1875.

Gathering and Transporting Supplies

Agent Clapp set his pencil in motion and remitted to the commissioner his estimate totaling exactly $15,000 for freighting goods, labor expense and finally erection of a new set of buildings.[172] Heavy reliance on his employees to quarry stone and lime, fabricate bricks and produce lumber for siding and roofing was evidenced in his budget. The agent ironed out fine details and was found advertising for seemingly insignificant but sorely needed items such as "horse and ox shoes," as well as larger outlays for mules, harnesses and one wagon.[173] Clapp hired a labor force of thirty to forty men consisting of mechanics, freighters and general work crews.[174]

Two options were at hand for transporting materials to the site: flatboats via the Yellowstone River or freighting by wagons. The appeal of the first may have waned when valuable materials were lost when one craft capsized

Agent Clapp's agency estimate. *Apr. 12, 1875, RG 75. Denver Archives.*

in the swollen Yellowstone River spring runoff.[175] Freighting by mule or ox teams on the other hand was a true-tried method. Hardy freighters, a bit rough around the collar, provided a more reliable means. One seasoned freighter was White Calfee, whose teams previously supplied Fort Parker with annuity goods. He often used four ten-mule teams; the "lead wagon was the biggest" and strongest, generally carrying 6,500 pounds. Calfee recalled the challenges. "Sometimes the axle broke. Then we had to unload and bind it together with sticks and ropes. Then again, the tongue would break." Mud was a real hardship, "often a regular mire," so much so they became buried "up to the hubs." His teams were particular and required a special touch. "Mules will not go without you swear[ing] at them." They are used to being "yelled at." Calfee clarified, "And the stronger you make it, the more they will do for you."[176]

Despite his skill, a few road improvements were necessary, especially in a difficult "mountain spur" eight miles east of Fort Parker. Clapp directed a road crew to hack this section out on May 19.[177] This was followed by wagons filled with "materials, tools and provisions."[178] Some of the first cargo included materials for the vital sawmill and adobe mill, the latter used for fashioning bricks.[179]

ABSAROKA AGENCY

As Clapp and his crew progressed eastward out of the canyon, they encountered high water on the Boulder River and impatiently waited two days before crossing safely. On May 29, a camp was made at the mouth of the Stillwater River opposite present Columbus, Montana.[180] Two days later, fording the Stillwater swollen by spring runoff, Clapp quipped, "Swiftwater would be more appropriate."[181]

The group then ascended the Stillwater Valley.[182] On May 31, 1875, Clapp enthusiastically wrote to his superiors described the new agency location: "We have I think a beautiful Site on a plain, apparently perfectly level, three miles long, and averaging one half mile in width. The East fork of the Rose Bud on one side and a Beaver Creek on the other. Both streams are lined with timber, and beyond them on each side is a high range of hills." He also noted a "rich loam soil" was found on the Rose Bud Creek bottoms. The stream would also be used for irrigation and to "supply the [saw]mill, stockade and barns with water," and eighteen miles distant near the foot of a mountain stood a supply of building materials consisting of

COL. J. I. ALLEN-SCOUT-1875

Left: Jirah Isham Allen. *Jim Annin Coll. MOB.*

Below: This deteriorated view of the agency depicts the usage of adobe brick. *2019-23-0001 MOB.*

"Pine Timber and Prairie Stone."[183] Best of all, the site, unlike Fort Parker, was "free from rocks and the terrible winds."[184]

Ground was broken on June 2, 1875. Eight days later, Clapp reported the sawmill was ready to use. It was powered by "a ditch 1¼ mile-long" and soon cut enough lumber for "a good corrall [*sic*]." The ditch would also supply livestock water and later "irrigate several hundred acres of land."

Housed temporarily in a partially constructed twenty-by-sixty-foot log barn, the crew worked their "utmost towards making this a model Agency."[185] The new agency was coined "Absaroka."[186]

Without delay, Clapp's "choice" laborers[187] completed a large foundation to support the two-hundred-by-twenty-five-foot warehouse.[188] This would function as a warehouse to store Crow annuity goods with adjacent issuing rooms for their distribution.[189] Four weeks later, adobe walls were set on the foundation.[190] The "walls had loop holes" for rifles, reminisced employee Jirah Allen. They were "not only built for protection, but the inside walls also served as the rear walls to the many rooms."[191]

By the end of July, Clapp's crew had also erected a blacksmith/carpenter's shop and seven residences, twenty-six by twenty-five feet. They had sawn "70,000 feet of lumber…burned seven to eight hundred bushels of lime, and…[fashioned] 80,000 adobe" bricks.[192] The brick process was explained by Allen. First, they "were molded and place[d] in a yard where the sun could dry them good and hard, and in a few days [they] were ready to go in place as walls of the different buildings." He was paid "50 bucks per month and board."[193]

HERE COME THE SIOUX

Aside from overseeing construction, Clapp also had a "multitude of things" that required his "personal attention." He found himself slipping behind in paperwork and correspondence duties and found it "impossible to keep the office work up."[194] However, these rather mundane duties had to pale in comparison to alarming news: "a fresh trail of a war party of about 100 Indians [were] bound apparently for the upper Yellowstone Country." In their path was the Absaroka Agency, new home to the Crow.[195]

A month after the first break in agency ground, an equally exciting but deadly set of events occurred at the new agency. On July 2, 1875, Clapp reported his timber camp was attacked near the mouth of the Stillwater by "about thirty Sioux" garbed "in war paint and dress." The employees were able to repel the warriors but at "great risk."[196] Not so fortunate was the fate of agency herder Jose Pablo Trojio,[197] known also as "Mexican Joe,"[198] who was ambushed and his horse stolen while trying to herd agency cattle. The little tributary where he was killed was later called Mexican Joe Creek.[199]

Further details were later reminisced by participant Tom Leforge: the "hostile attack upon our loggers occurred six or seven miles downstream from Absaroka. Eight or ten of us were in camp there, getting out timbers for additional agency buildings." Ox teams had been turned out at the end of the day to graze, "looped" together in pairs, as were the horses, to "hinder" thieves, he explained. When cattle went missing, Leforge observed agency employees, Tom Stewart and Mexican Joe, "hurrying" them from six pursing Sioux. Shots then rang out in the direction of Leforge, who recalled one member of his party had fashioned around his neck "a bootleg, cut off and sewed together," filled with a "weighty supply" of cartridges.[200] The apparatus proved lifesaving during a two-hour "exchange of shots" between Leforge, Mitch Boyer and the Sioux. During the fracas, White Calfee was wounded in the thumb[201] and "Mexican Joe" came up missing.

The following afternoon, Clapp and party investigated the scene and found near the banks of the Stillwater River a piece of Mexican Joe's scalp, his stockings and moccasins.[202] "The poor man evidently made a brave fight for his life," he concluded. His body was not recovered, but articles "distinctively of Sioux manufacture"[203] consisting of "one nickel revolver marked (xx) (a), one pair of moccasins, one fine telescope, two hats, pipe stem ec [sic]" were found.[204] Found also in the aftermath of Mexican Joe's death were "two small tents, that were made of flour sacks." They bore the stamp "Anchor Mills XXX Flour, St. Louis, Inspected for Indian Department, F.S. Clarkston Inspector," implying the annuity flour sacks were repurposed and left by the Lakota Sioux.[205]

The saga at the agency continued near midnight on July 4 when a trio of trappers weary from an Indian ambush escaped for refuge.[206] Clapp did not believe their story,[207] however, and at "2½ o'clock a.m." the night was interrupted by "the entire herd" of corralled horses and mules "driven off at full speed by the Indians." Pursuit was attempted, but the thieves "planned so skillfully, and being strong…got away clean and clear."[208] Efforts to safeguard the cattle were thwarted by large "numbers" of Sioux appearing east of the agency along bluffs "saluting" the employees with several shots.[209]

Clapp was resentful of the military based at Fort Ellis just east of Bozeman, Montana. They refused to provide protection at the agency during construction.[210] He was informed the post's duty was to guard the citizens and settlements in the surrounding Gallatin Valley. Clapp concluded the agency was left intentionally unprotected by officers upset it was relocated about ninety miles farther[211] from their post and therefore more dangerous. [212] He chided their incompetency and lack of ability even to "defend the people of Gallatin Valley." The numerous "graves of murdered men, scattered all over the hills from [the agency] to Fort Ellis"

Top: Fort Ellis, established in 1867, became the home of the Second Regiment, U.S. Cavalry. *Denver Public Library Special Collections.*

Bottom: Crow scout, by Edward Curtis. *loc.gov/item/2002722308.*

were in his estimation proof of their inadequacy and a need for "efficient action."[213] He was convinced it was the Crow scouts who kept the Gallatin and Yellowstone Valleys residents safe and "the means to stopping three war parties."[214] They scouted against the Sioux for many reasons; not only was the tribe very numerous but also aggressive against them. But in cooperating with the whites, the Crow gained protection and possible trade advantages during the height of intertribal warfare.[215]

Though Clapp was confident he could protect the agency, he was reluctant and displeased about sending his own workforce to do the job of the military, knowing it would "seriously interfere" with his budget and ability to build the agency timely.[216]

GOVERNOR BENJAMIN F. POTTS

Clapp's pleas for military aid went unheeded. When news spread of the agency depredations, it triggered Montana territorial governor Benjamin F. Potts. Although the governor was not an advocate of the new agency location, he became enraged on learning Clapp's request for Fort Ellis troop protection was "refused" due to there being "no troops to spare." Potts churned; Montana citizens were "clamorous for protection," yet he was "powerless" to provide them. He rebuked District Commander of Montana Colonel Gibbons for keeping "nearly all of his troops" at Fort Shaw, where no Indian raids had occurred since 1869. Then he complained of this conduct to Gibbons's superior, General Sheridan, in "hope" his sway would secure troops.[217] His accusation over the lack of military assistance both at the agency and the Gallatin Valley was also directed to Secretary of the Interior Columbus Delano. The outspoken governor deemed Fort Ellis soldiers "powerless" to protect the Gallatin Valley or "defend their own Fort."[218] Potts's letters made their way to President Ulysses Grant and other high-ranking military officials. A chagrined General Alfred Terry, commander of Department of Dakota (including Montana), found the statements "unjust" and "erroneous" and recommended Potts leave military matters to the those with proper "knowledge" and "disposition."[219] Military officials had more to worry about than Potts, namely, apprehension of a full-scale war with the Sioux "at a time" when troops were "not prepared for it."[220] Troops in Montana Territory were insufficient and found scattered at Missouri River ports to stem the flow of whiskey trade, as guards along the Carroll Trail or on scouting and reconnaissance missions.[221]

THE LAKOTA AGAIN

Impervious to the mudslinging and problems of the U.S. government, the Lakota again targeted the agency, home to their old foe the Crow, with a summer series of raiding. Beginning on July 21, 1875, a wagon train belonging to Bozeman's Nelson Story was attacked in the Stillwater Valley about six miles from the agency. With Nelson's party was U.S. Indian detective Captain Andrew Dusold, fired on by two Indians at forty yards, but he was unharmed. Story's men pursed the hostiles, finding "saddles, clothing and trinkets which they had stripped off for the fight." They were given a verbal warning by the Lakota, interpreted by Story's employee Mitch Bouyer, as a "large" camp was coming and they "would give us plenty of fight."[222] This same day, one of the agency herders was ambushed a mile and a half from the agency; his horse and forty-three head of cattle were taken. Story, Dusold and seventeen men pursued the raiders for over twenty miles toward the Clark's Fork River. Nine head of cattle were recovered and eight found dead. A week later, two more cowboys were targeted by the Lakota. The incident resulted in the death of agency night herder James Hilderbrand. His companion scurried behind some rocks until help arrived from the agency. On August 1, an agency employee and his companion who were sent from the agency were also attacked.[223] Clapp reported, "All hostile Indians disappeared from the neighborhood there is no knowing at what moment they may re-appear."[224] Even less definite was the effect the Lakota hostilities had on Crow morale as they witnessed their hereditary enemy plunder with inconsequential suppression efforts. The agent believed this was a great barrier toward teaching farming pursuits and general advancements.[225]

In the midst of the all the calamity, Clapp had nearly expended his agency building funds.[226] The hostile attacks, he explained, "hindered our work" and set it back by an estimated $4,000. He sent an amended budget[227] for construction of a corral, 100 by 150 feet, and adobe stable walls; six 130 by 16 feet adobe Indian homes; and an interpreter's house, 50 by 20 feet. To serve as "council-room, office and additional quarters," the fourth lateral 150 by 23 feet was under construction, as were the adobe walls for a two-story building, 30 by 30 feet. Despite the setbacks, he proudly reported in September "all articles entering into the construction of the building have been produced by the agency-employees, with the exception of window-sashes, doors, nails, locks, and other similar articles." He asserted the agency buildings are "of a permanent character…the best of any public building in the Territory."[228] Construction had just been completed when the Mountain Crow "arrived en masse at the Agency…[and] expressed themselves as satisfied and please[d] with the place."[229]

LAND EXCHANGE

While Agent Clapp was preoccupied with relocating and building the new Crow Agency, traders at Bensons Landing were also on the move. They packed up their wares, following down the Yellowstone River. They set up shops within twelve to fifteen miles from the reservation boundary, as close they could possibly get to the agency. "Whiskey selling, gambling, and horse thieving have been carried out to an astonishing extent," Clapp stressed.[230] The thought of these potential dens of inebriation so near his charges launched his crusade to force the traders out of business. His concern was not over the agency itself; it was isolated, "far toward the interior of the Reservation [and] as good a place as can be found." The trouble lay in the fact the Crow would often pass by the traders' camps on their way to hunt in the Judith Basin. In order to protect them from undue influence and spirits, Clapp requested the government set aside a "belt of territory twenty miles wide on the north bank of the Yellowstone River, from Big Timber Creek to the meridian, eastern line of the Crow Reservation." Setting this section apart from Indian County was critical not only to the Crow, he levered, but "the peace of Eastern Montana."[231] When word leaked out, a firestorm erupted, including the fury of trader Horace Countryman. Clapp deemed him "utterly unfit to be in an Indian country—a man of bad character and of infamous reputation."[232] Countryman located just across the Yellowstone River and became one of the "confederates" who pressed to stop the land exchange and reopen the country north of the river.[233]

Weighing in on the matter, the outspoken Governor B.F. Potts rationalized the near proximity of the new agency to the Yellowstone River will "afford traders the same opportunity" as did the old agency.[234] The "alleged reason"

Horace Countryman. *Jim Annin Coll. MOB.*

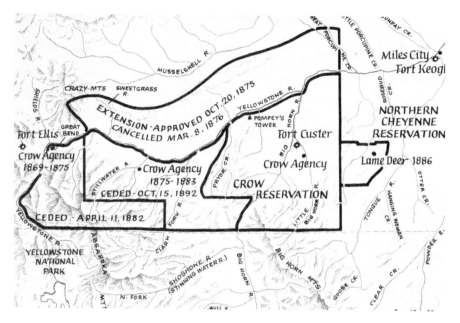

The land exchange. *From* Plainsmen of the Yellowstone *by G.P. Putnam's Sons, imprint of Penguin Publishing Group, a division of Penguin Random House LLC.*

for the land extension was identical to the reason the Crow were removed in the first place. Fort Parker was too near the reservation border, tempting travel into Gallatin County where the Crow "traded for whiskey." The land extension, predicted Potts, "will not remedy the evil" of the whiskey trade.[235] By granting the extension, the governor foresaw future settlement in the area would become limited. Not only was it the surveyed route of the Northern Pacific Railroad, jeopardizing pending construction, but halting construction of a wagon road leading from Bozeman to eastern markets. The governor explained to the secretary of interior this was "good agricultural and grazing land with many settlers and large herds of cattle" already occupying it who would be deprived of all benefits.[236] Others protested that if the belt of land in Gallatin County was removed, it would jeopardize "the integrity" of the county. A "considerable" number of citizens felt this way, including Horace Countryman,[237] prompting the trader to circulate his petition "against the severance from Gallatin… for the benefit, practically or theoretically, of the Crow Indians."[238] The document was endorsed by Governor Potts and Delegate Martin Maginnis.[239] Despite the resistance, an executive order created on October

20, 1875, withdrew the public land, setting apart for usage by the Crow Indians the described tract of country situated in Montana Territory and adding to their reservation, viz:

> *Commencing at a point in the mid channel of the Yellowstone River where the 107th degree of west longitude crosses the said river; thence up said mid channel of the Yellowstone to the mouth of Big Timber creek; thence up said creek twenty miles, if the said creek can be followed that distance; if not, then in the same direction continued from the source thereof, to a point twenty miles from the mouth of said creek; thence eastwardly along a line parallel to the Yellowstone, no point of which shall be less than twenty miles from the river, to the 107th degree of west longitude; thence south to the place of beginning.[240]*

Word of the new order created a citizen's uproar as headlined in one local news source, "An Obnoxious Encroachment."[241] Bozeman residents quickly rallied with a meeting between notables, including ex-agent Fellows Pease, Nelson Story, Judge Davis, Honorable R.P. Vivion and the instigator, Agent Clapp. Clapp spoke of past troubles with whiskey and traders at Fort Parker and "similar" issues at the new agency. The land buffer, he assured, would serve only as a "preventive measure." Settlers did not need to relocate, nor would travel on the Yellowstone River corridor be restricted. He emphasized the order would not "retard the progress of civilization, settlement or future prosperity of Eastern Montana."[242]

Concerned citizens expressed a different view to President Grant, believing development and occupancy the ticket to "settle the wild Indian question."[243] They submitted their petition to the president against the executive order, "praying" he would rescind it.[244] With pressures mounting against the order, Agent Clapp suggested an amendment to ensure unencumbered river travel.[245] Not only was the request denied, but the entire short-lived extension was also revoked by President Grant on March 9, 1876. Secretary of the Interior Zachariah Chandler clarified the annexation was "solely for the purpose of terminating the pernicious traffic in liquors carried on with the Indians." This was not the solution, and he suggested "citizens of Montana and the Legislative Assembly work…to enact laws to subserve the purpose."[246]

This left "Countryman and his confederates" unencumbered along the Yellowstone River and free to peddle whiskey. "It will be a sad day for both Crows and whites," exclaimed Clapp. "To say nothing of the murders and outrages which will inevitably result." He predicted this would "demoralize the Crows," offsetting any "beneficence" provided by himself or the government."[247] Chief Blackfoot was of the same mind. At his request, his words on the matter were written down by Clapp for submission to the president. The Crow leader feared that if the whiskey traders were allowed near the reservation, "some of his young men would go there and get crazy and bad. Then some one would be killed and trouble come."[248]

Fort Pease

During Clapp's tenure, a scheme was promoted by Bozeman residents involving the heart of the Yellowstone Valley. Though it did not directly affect the Crow at the agency, it did negatively influence the stabilization of the valley and morale of the Crow. Former Crow agent Fellows Pease and employee Zadok (Zed) Daniels along with Bozeman businessman Paul McCormick envisioned a frontier settlement and trading post near the confluence of the Big Horn and Yellowstone Rivers, one hundred miles east of the agency. Firm in their beliefs as additional steamboat traffic materialized, the trio spearheaded Fort Pease, confident it would become an important factor in the economic life of Montana Territory. Trade in furs and peltries was their announced objective. However, an advertisement in the November 1875 issue in Bozeman's *Avant Courier* directed to "hunters, trappers and miners" suggested further insight into the partners' motive.

Seeds for this frontier post may have developed when Pease was Crow agent at Fort Parker. Undoubtedly, he was aware of lucrative profits traders gained from Indian exchange. Another key factor was the high regard the Crow held for him. It was also well-known Pease held "more influence with the Crows than any white man living.…They will do anything that he advises" expressed one military official.[249] For his venture to become successful, Pease would need heavy reliance on Crow participation to obtain furs and potentially serve as middlemen for other tribes. There was one obstacle that could hinder success, namely, the bitter intertribal warfare between the Sioux and the Crow. In regard to the latter, Pease was said to have "expressed a great desire that peace should be established between the Crows and Sioux."[250] This rhetoric was opposed by miliary officials fearing "encouraging peace between our friendly indians [sic] and those deadly hostile[s]…may be philanthropy to the indians [sic] but it is death to the whites."[251] The potential resulting alliance between the tribes could ultimately overpower government forces.[252] Tensions had already mounted between the tribes. Even though their reservation was hundreds of miles to the east, the Lakota were triggered by Crow and settlers' intrusion into the prime hunting grounds of the Yellowstone Valley. The stage was set for a full-scale war between the foes.

Organizational goals stated Fort Pease would benefit frontier communities by improving trade routes from Bozeman eastward along the Yellowstone River to the mouth of the Tongue River (then thought to be the head of navigation on the Yellowstone River). However, rumors of rich mineral deposits in the area were no doubt a motive for those involved. Under this shroud, on June 17, 1875, a crew of twenty men launched into the Yellowstone River with three boats: the *Bozeman*, *Maggie Hoppy* and the *Prairie Belle*. A party of seventeen proceeded overland with intentions of uniting at the Stillwater River. The trip was barely underway when the *Bozeman* struck a snag, losing invaluable supplies and arms. An all-day search recovered only three guns and a cannon. The following day near the mouth of the Stillwater River, the *Prairie Belle* met a similar misfortune. When the overland group assembled, they once again struck out.

Near the approximate time Pease was going down the river, the Crow left the Absaroka Agency for their annual summer hunt. They proceeded down the north bank of the Yellowstone River to nine miles below the mouth of the Big Horn River, a point they "do not usually go…[and] have not been below for the past five years." One military officer was "confident [the Crow] were induced to go this year by Major Pease," who was expected to join them there but was delayed. The Crow arrival was greeted instead by a Sioux attack and ensuing three-day battle.[253] Thus, when Pease and the overland party finally reached the mouth of the Big Horn, they found the bluffs lined with Sioux. He must have realized then his plans for conciliatory trade between the tribes was out of the question and prospects for success had dimmed with the recent battle.

On the twenty-fourth, three miles below the mouth of the Big Horn River, the boats safely landed on the north side of the Yellowstone River. Here, the men quickly constructed a stockade approximately 235 feet square. Three sides of it were enclosed with log houses and the other with poles.[254] Pease stayed long enough to oversee initial fort construction, leaving the fourth day when he and two others started downriver. Pease was bound for the East with plans to later return to Bozeman; however, his strategy did not materialize, as there would be no more steamboats on the Yellowstone that year, thus leaving others to carry on the Fort Pease project.[255]

Almost immediately, the hunters from Fort Pease became an irritation even to the friendly Crow, for they reduced game, meaning fewer furs and pelts for either party to trade. Particularly offensive was their procedure of poisoning carcasses to bait and kill wolves for pelts. Crow peoples believed wolves to be cunning and clever, productive and problem-solving.[256] Imitating wolf behaviors, Crow scouts dressed in wolf hide, painting their bodies with mud to take on the dull color of wolves. The leader of the scouts was called *cheetissaahke*, "old man wolf," due to his experience and leadership abilities.[257] The hunters' disregard for the sacred animal earned only the contempt of the Crow.

However, Crow reactions were mild compared to the hostile Lakota Indians who claimed the territory as their own, thus attacking the post and the intruders at every opportunity.[258] It became difficult to protect the fort. "I can't get no one to stand guard, all [would] rather work," claimed one participant.[259] The hostility over the presence of Fort Pease extended hundreds of miles beyond the fort. On July 10, a trio of men—Sam Shively, Patrick Hyde and Nelson Weaver—departed the fort westbound for Bozeman but were attacked in the vicinity of the Stillwater River. Shively was killed. Weaver and the wounded Hyde, accompanied by Henry Countryman, traveled all night to reach the Absaroka Agency, where Dr. A.J. Hunter treated Hyde's nonfatal wounds. Two days later, Paul McCormick, now first in command at Fort Pease, narrowly escaped death when he and James Edward were suddenly fired on. McCormick's horse took a bullet in the flank, causing it to buck and run, but the rider hung on and made for the stockade. Edwards was shot and killed. The incident compelled McCormick to send a courier to the *Bozeman Times* requesting guns and supplies.[260] Bozeman citizens responded promptly with a boat aptly named the *Rescue*. The group was fired on by the Lakota near Pryor Creek, and then their craft capsized near the Big Horn River. Cannon salute from the Big Horn Gun was a welcomed summons as the rescue party arrived on July 29. Ansel Hubbel made a return trip to Fort Pease on August 16 with more supplies.[261]

Events at the fort quieted until August 28, when a party of trappers was attacked, injuring one. With the onset of winter, the Lakota resumed their attacks, hampering abilities of those within the fort to hunt for meat or trap for furs and skins. Two attempting to do so, Fred Harlan and Orrin Mason, were killed nearby. Mason's two companions eventually reached safety at the Absaroka Agency. Another round of attacks at Fort Pease the first week of the New Year left five men wounded, Patrick Sweeny fatally. Evening the score, a party of Crow led by Bear Wolf spotted eight Lakota watching

Above: Se-ta-pit-se (Packs the Bear or Bear Wolf) and wife, "Stays with the Horses." *BAE GN 03380A*.

Opposite: Symbiotic of the value and relationship between the Crow and horse is *Crow Indian on the Lookout*, 1858–60, Alfred Jacob Miller. *Walters Art Museum*.

the fort and "killed six or seven."[262] Bear Wolf's deft skills and prowess are clearly represented by his wife's elk tooth dress.[263]

By the end of January, prospects looked dim, and the bright future for the fort vanished. News promising gold in the Black Hills reached Fort Pease, enticing Benjamin Dexter and seventeen men to head westbound for supplies at Bozeman. Stopping first at Fort Ellis, the party handed the military commander a signed petition requesting troops "to check the havoc of these hostile Sioux."[264] McCormick also made a fast trip to Bozeman, where, joining Dexter, the pair painted a picture of despair for the remaining men in the fort, even though they had chosen to stay. The duo went further and accused Agent Clapp of inciting the Crow to harass the post, thus forcing its closure.[265] In reality, the savvy Dexter and McCormick's probable objective was to persuade the military to evacuate Fort Pease, loading and transporting all remaining goods and supplies at government expense. The ploy worked.[266]

Seven days into his new command at Fort Ellis, Major James Brisbin telegraphed General Alfred Terry for permission to relieve Fort Pease. Orders came in mid-February and found troops departing Fort Ellis. Near the present town of Columbus, Montana, Brisbin halted to gain recruits at the Absaroka Agency. "Get all the Indians and white men you can together and join me on the road."[267] As incentive, he added the Crow could keep "all the ponies captured."[268] This lure was attractive to the Crow. According to Plenty Coups, the horse and rider were one, and retaining a large horse herd provided more likelihood of owning a prized horse. The rare buffalo horse, with his speed and canny, could feed and clothe a family and bring honors in war. A problem horse could potentially kill, maim or cause shame.[269]

Also on the officer's mind was the possibility of giving Sitting Bull and the Sioux a "set back." "Get out every Crow warrior and employee you can," he emphasized.[270] On February 27, Brisbin gained thirty Crow and twenty-five citizens. Twenty-four additional Crow led by Thin Belly and Good Heart joined the following morning.[271]

Arriving at Fort Pease on March 5, the relief party located only nineteen men, some reluctant to leave. No Lakota were discovered in the vicinity, although tipis and heavily traveled trails were found. Two days later, the fort was evacuated, and troops returned to Fort Ellis on March 17, 1876, having traveling 398 miles.[272] Brisbin's greatest effect was not in evacuating the fort but in broadening his commander General Alfred Terry's understanding of how to best utilize troops for an upcoming campaign with hostile Sioux and Northern Cheyenne.[273]

For the Crow, their willingness to aid the military was another show of good faith toward the United States, but the failure at Fort Pease demonstrated the Lakota Sioux ability of overpowering and outwitting them.

4

SCOUTS AND BATTLES

The End of the Peace Policy

As warfare tensions mounted between Plains tribes and western immigrants, events in the nation's capital moved toward resolving the issue of Indians who refused to settle on their reservations, particularly the Lakota Sioux. It had been seven years since the signing of the treaty of 1868, guaranteeing a permanent reservation and assimilation strategies to funnel them into American society. A majority did live on the reservation. But a plan was devised targeting those who roamed off—especially during winter—with hope of sustaining themselves in the traditional manner by hunting.

The dismantling of President Grant's Peace Policy prompted an ultimatum issued on December 16, 1875. The order instructed Indian agents to deem any Indian who had not submitted to reservation life by January 31, 1876, be considered as hostile, granting military authority to deal with those who did not. The plan lay within the army conducting a winter campaign to engage dissident Indians before warmer weather enabled reservation Indians to join them. Orders were given for General George Crook to march from Fort Fetterman, near present-day Douglas, Wyoming. To aid Crook, Lieutenant Colonel George Armstrong Custer would depart from Fort Abraham Lincoln, Dakota Territory. However, due to logistical problems caused by winter and political issues, only Crook's forces were able to get in the field. His command did strike a blow: the first major combat in what became known as the Great Sioux War occurred on March 17, 1876, against a small village of Sioux and Northern Cheyenne winter roamers along the Powder River. The encounter alerted the Natives of the necessity for consolidation of their villages to survive. On the military end, it forced Crook out of the field and back to Fort Fetterman for supplies, thus ending the winter campaign designed for surprise attacks.[274]

Almost three months after the Powder River fight, Crook again struck north from Fort Fetterman. He was one of three military columns whose strategy was conceived by General Philip H. Sheridan. The Dakota Column, under the command of General Alfred Terry, consisted mainly of the Seventh U.S. Cavalry led by Lieutenant Colonel George Armstrong Custer, while Colonel John Gibbon, head of the "Montana Column," patrolled the Yellowstone River. The columns were to converge on the Powder River–Yellowstone region where Sitting Bull, Crazy Horse and other non-treaty Sioux roamed.

INDIAN SCOUTS

One of the many challenges for the army on the frontier was locating bands of hostile Indians. The primary way was through army patrols, but with the military's limited manpower, experience and overall lack of familiarity with the lay of the land, Indian foes had an advantage. The army recognized the need for means to think and scout like an Indian. With this in mind, in 1867 Congress gave authorization for the army to enlist Indians as scouts for short but renewable terms of service. Enlisted Indian scouts were mustered usually for six months; paid the regular thirteen dollars per month; uniformed, armed and provided rations like regulars; and generally under the charge of a junior officer designated chief of scouts.[275]

The Crow were fully cognizant, as well as indignant, about the Lakota Sioux takeover in their coveted Yellowstone Valley. The Sioux are a large tribe, acknowledged Blackfoot in an earlier statement, but "we are not afraid of them. They want to come on our land, but we intend to keep them off."[276] The view of retaining Crow homeland was compelling. Two Belly, a River Crow leader, affirmed if the Sioux "were not driven off, the land we wanted for our children would be stolen."[277] Another Crow leader, Iron Bull, proclaimed, "I love all white men. The Sioux, Cheyenne, and Arapahoes do not....If you do not know it; I tell you so."[278]

Crow pledges of loyalty and faithfulness were offered to the white man who dominated in sheer numbers, trade items and much-needed firepower.[279] Thus, the military considered the recruitment of Crow scouts for the Great Sioux War an "ideal" choice. They were intimate with the territory and longtime foes of the Cheyenne and Sioux.[280] They also "understood to fight the whites would only lead to self-destruction, but more importantly to drive out their old foes would ensure a peaceful future for the Crow people."[281]

Enlisting Crow Scouts

Riding through eighteen inches of wet snow, Colonel John Gibbon, head of the "Montana Column," arrived at the Absaroka Agency on April 8, 1876. Escorting him were Lieutenant James H. Bradley, Major James S. Brisbin, Captain Henry Freeman and Lieutenant Levi Burnett. They were quickly provided housing by Agent Clapp. The following morning, Gibbon enacted the provision authorizing U.S. Army enlistment of Indians as scouts. Gibbon's principal objective was to recruit twenty-five warriors for the ensuing campaign in what would be later called the Great Sioux War. This campaign, like the preceding winter one, was directed against Lakota and Northern Cheyenne bands who had not heeded the government ultimatum to return to their reservation agencies.

Avid historian and journal keeper Lieutenant James H. Bradley, Seventh Infantry, was given command of the Crow scouts. In his memoir, *The March of the Montana Column*, Bradley described the enlistment at the April 9, 1876 Crow council with Gibbon. Among the principal leaders present were Blackfoot, Thin Belly, Iron Bull, Bull That Goes Hunting, Shows His Face, Medicine Wolf, Old Onion, Mountain Pocket, Crane In The Sky, Sees All Over the Land, One Feather, Spotted Horse, Long Snake, Frog, Small Beard, Curly, Shot In The Jaw, White Forehead, Old Crow, Old Dog, White Mouth and Crazy Head. Pierre Chien (spelled several ways, Chene, Chane, Shane) was their interpreter.

Lieutenant James Bradley. *MHS 941-317.*

After cordialities, General Gibbon got to the point:

> *I have come down here to make war on the Sioux. The Sioux are your enemy and ours. For a long while they have been killing white men and killing Crows. I am going to punish the Sioux for making war upon the white man. If the Crows want to make war upon the Sioux, now is their time. If they want to drive them from their country and prevent them from sending war parties into their country to murder their men, now is their time. If they want to get revenge for the Crows that have fallen, to get revenge for the killing of such men as the gallant soldier, Long Horse, now is the time.*[282]

Crook explained he was looking for twenty-five "young, active brave men" to be "soldiers of the Government" in exchange for pay and food.[283] When Gibbon reacted to their silence and noncommitment, Old Crow retorted, "Don't be too fast," as they were thinking. Blackfoot, conferring with the Crow in "animated" and "impressive gestures," then came forward to speak:

> *The white people want us to assist them. I do not know the ways of the whites, my people do not know their ways. The land we tread belongs to us, and we want our children always to dwell in it. All other Indian tribes do evil to the whites, but I and my people hold fast to them with love. We want our reservation to be large, we want to go on eating buffalo, and so we hold fast to the whites.*[284]

Blackfoot clarified he could not compel his warriors to join the troops but hoped they would go. A skeptical Iron Bull recalled during construction of the agency the Crow "begged" the agents to help fight the Sioux, but instead the Crow "fought them alone." This wizened leader pointed out the Crow had their own "way of going to war. If our young men seek the Sioux, they travel night and day till they find them" and then return home. "The Sioux are a very strong people, a very brave people," added Old Crow. "Will you believe what our young men tell you [about them]?…They will not lie to you."[285]

The council diverged into complaints about lack of food and ammunition, compelling Gibbon to remark that those who joined him would receive plenty of both.

The following morning, Lieutenant Bradley enlisted twenty-three Crows. He swore them in using a point of a knife, an act the Crow considered a binding obligation. He gave them each a red band of cloth about six inches wide to be worn above their left elbow to be used to distinguish them from enemy warriors. Bradley observed that the recruits were predominately less than thirty years of age, but two men were over sixty. They had their own arms, good breechloaders. One had only a revolver and the other, bow and arrow. Also hired were two white men, Barney Bravo and "LeForgey," who both lived among the Crow for several years and would serve as interpreters.[286] "LeForgey," was Tom Leforge, also known as "Horse Rider." Mitch Bouyer was hired as a guide.

Amid a heavy snowfall with accumulations of eighteen inches, Gibbon, staff and the Crow scouts departed the Absaroka Agency on April 11 to rejoin the Montana Column. Lieutenant Bradley was given command of the scouts. Their first shock to army life came the next day when Bradley insisted the Crow participate in reveille. Leforge suggested he let the Crow follow their own routine or they might refuse to serve. The column reached the former site of Fort Pease and remained there for over three weeks due to military delays with Custer and Crook. During that time, they had not seen any hostile Indians, but apparently, they were near. Thirty-two horses were stolen from the Crow, including one belonging to Leforge.[287]

Orders finally set Gibbon's Montana Column into motion to proceed for the mouth of the Rosebud River, but upon arrival, they again waited several weeks for Terry's delayed Dakota Column. Nearly three weeks after leaving

Tom Leforge pictured in 1926 with his biographer, Thomas Baily Marquis. *Author photo.*

Fort Shaw, Gibbon connected with General Terry on June 9. This same week, the third column, with General Crook's troops, marched north from Fort Fetterman.

The Battle of the Rosebud

Near present-day Sheridan, Wyoming, Crook's Crow and Shoshone scouts appeared. Old Crow, Medicine Crow and Good Heart led the 176-Crow contingency.[288] Lieutenant John G. Bourke, an aide to General Crook, was present when the Crow scouts rode into camp. His impressions of them are retold in *On the Border with Crook*:

> *The Crow Indians, perhaps as a consequence of their residence among the elevated banks and cool, fresh mountain ranges between the Big Horn River and the Yellowstone are somewhat fairer than the other tribes about them; they are all above medium height, not a few being quite tall, and many have a noble expression of countenance. Their dress consisted of a shirt of flannel, cotton, or buckskin; breech-clout; leggings of blanket; moccasins of deer, elk, or buffalo hide; coat of bright-colored blanket, made with loose sleeves and hood; and a head-dress fashioned in diverse shapes, but most frequently formed from an old black army hat, with the top cut out and sides bound round with feathers, fur, and scarlet cloth. Their arms were all breech loaders, throwing cartridges of caliber .50 with an occasional .45. Lances, medicine-poles, and tomahawks figured in the procession. The tomahawks, made of long knives inserted in shafts or handles of wood and horn, were murderous weapons. Accompanying these Indians were a few little boys, whose business was to hold horses and other unimportant work while their elders conducted the dangerous operations of the campaign.[289]*

That evening, beside an "immense fire," Crook outlined his plans to them. "These are our lands," the seasoned leader Old Crow replied. "The Great Spirit gave them to our fathers, but the Sioux stole them from us. They hunt upon our mountains. They fish in our streams. They have stolen our horses. We want back our lands."[290]

The following morning, June 17, Crook marched his column of one-thousand-plus soldiers and scouts toward the headwaters of the Rosebud River. He "was bristling for a fight."[291] Crook was unprepared for the organized attack from warriors led by Lakota Chief Crazy Horse and

Left: Crow scout. *981-086 MHS*.

Below: The Grand Council, Goose Creek, June 15, 1876. *From* Frank Leslie's Illustrated Newspaper, *September 2, 1876. loc.gov/pictures/resource/cph.3b02596/*.

Cheyenne Chief Two Moon. Intense fighting marked the six-to-eight-hour Battle of the Rosebud. Crook's troops withdrew. Eight days later, because Crook's troops were forced from the war zone to resupply, they were not available to support Lieutenant Colonel George A. Custer and his troops on the banks of the Little Bighorn.[292]

Custer's Crow Scouts

Days after the Battle of the Rosebud, Lieutenant Colonel George Armstrong Custer with the Seventh Cavalry arrived at the mouth of the Rosebud River. Custer's own scouts were unfamiliar with the territory. Lieutenant Bradley detached his "six best men" to go with Custer: Goes Ahead, Hairy Moccasin, Curly, White Man Runs Him, Half Yellow Face and White Swan.[293] Curly, the youngest, was about sixteen or seventeen. In a letter to his wife, Libby, Custer was impressed. "I now have some Crow scouts with me, as they are familiar with the country. They are magnificent looking men, so much handsomer and more Indian-like than any we have ever seen, and so jolly and sportive, nothing of the gloomy, silent Redman about them."[294]

After leaving the Rosebud, Custer followed a trail leading to a large hostile Indian encampment on the Little Big Horn River. Events unfolded on June 25, 1876, that ultimately led to the Battle of the Little Bighorn.

During the siege on what is now called Reno Hill, forty-nine soldiers met their death with five more dying later due to wounds. Quite possibly more would have perished if it weren't for the valor of the Crow scouts present. White Swan, while trying to defend, was shot in his right hand and wrist, right thigh and knee. He also took a blow to the head. Hairy Moccasin was credited for rescuing one of Major Reno's men.[295] Half Yellow Face, also called Half His Face Painted Yellow (Ischu Shi Dish) or Big Belly,[296] willingly, under heavy fire, filled canteens for the parched and wounded from the Little Big Horn River, five hundred yards down a steep hill.[297]

Unaware of the previous day's battle on the Little Big Horn River, Lieutenant Bradley was ordered on a scouting mission. He soon discovered something was amiss upon finding personal articles he recognized as belonging to Custer's Crow scouts. Noticing three men watching, he attempted to communicate via smoke and blanket signals. Cautiously, a trio— Goes Ahead, Hairy Moccasin and White Man Runs Him—approached him. Sharing the news of the demise with Bradley's scout, Little Face and others suddenly "shouted out at the top of their voices a doleful series of cries and wails." The scouts were the first to hear of the death of Custer and his men. Bradley noted, "Little Face in particular wept with a bitterness of anguish."[298] Declining the troop's invitation to travel with them, the Crow scouts and interpreter Bravo departed for the Absaroka Agency.[299]

Controversy remains, but at some point during the battle, Curly rode easterly into the Rosebud Valley, then southerly, where General Terry and Colonel Gibbon remained aboard the *Far West*. After three days of traveling, he eventually located the steamer at the mouth of the Little Big Horn River. He approached but was unable to communicate his message to those aboard, so Curly resorted to drawing what he witnessed, a few dots that represented white men, surrounded by more dots to represent Indians.

It was not until June 29 that a dispatch to the *Far West* brought the first clear news that the Lakota and Northern Cheyenne warriors overtook Custer and his 263 soldiers at Little Bighorn. The steamer was ordered to prepare for the wounded troopers.[300]

Lieutenant Bradley returned to report Custer's death to General Terry and Colonel Gibbon. Their response was disbelief, "blank faces, and silent

White Man Runs Him, Hairy Moccasin and Goes Ahead in 1908 on the now named Little Bighorn Battlefield. *Author photo.*

In 1878, White married the Crow daughter of Crooked Foot, Yoho na ho or Julia. The couple had six children. Jim Annin Coll. *MOB*.

tongues."[301] The troops then marched to the mouth of the Little Big Horn for the task of burying the dead. One involved with this duty was William H. White, a mule packer in Troop F with Colonel Gibbon. Using tipi lodge poles and buffalo robes left behind from the fleeing hostiles, litters were constructed for transport.[302]

Volumes have been written on the battle. Emphasis here is to note the dichotomy and confusion the Crow were subjected to during this period. On one hand, Crow agents urged them to undertake farming methods and settle down. The next request was to take up arms to defend their homeland. One outcome of the battle was due to the fact of Curly bearing the news of Custer and the troops demise to General Terry[303] Curly became highly sought after for interviews, photographs and parades, a favorite of early frontier photographers, for he was not only photogenic but also, it seems, amenable to having his picture taken often. The jacket is also picturesque but likely a prop, as this was not the Crow style of design at this period.[304]

After the battle, Terry with fifty Crow scouts joined forces with Colonel Nelson A. Miles's unit and set out in search of the fleeing Sioux and

Lakota. They were joined by General Crook. Throughout the remainder of the summer of 1876 and into the winter of 1877, the military pursued and engaged in combat against the non-treaty Indians. By the end of the summer of 1877, General Miles, assisted at times by four hundred auxiliary Crow, had tracked down remaining pockets of dissidents.

Curly (Shi-Shia). *H-00938 Haynes Coll. MHS.*

Return to the Absaroka Agency

The Crow, for the first time in decades, were now relatively free from being in a constant readiness in case of attack on their own domain.[305] Agent Clapp was hopeful they could finally settle in and work at supporting themselves as farmers and herders.[306] A small pocket, predominantly men married to Crow women, requested acreage allowed to them under the terms of the 1868 treaty. They included Alex Hundley, Thomas Shane, Charles Fisher, H.A. Searles, Rock Berthiaume, E. Williamson, Thomas Kent, H.L. Williams, B. Bravo, Thomas Stewart, Joseph Hill, J.P. Fox and others. In a proposal sent to Commissioner of Indian Affairs John Q. Smith, they also suggested the government purchase their "surplus" crops and produce at market prices.[307] The suggestion was looked on favorably, for it was reasoned relatives of the Crow women would pitch in to help promote and encourage farming efforts.[308] However, before Clapp could see results, Lewis H. Carpenter took charge as the new Crow agent on October 21, 1876.[309]

5

AGENTS JAMES CARPENTER AND GEORGE FROST

The Indian Agent

It was widely held that the "most important duties in the conduct of Indian affairs" were performed by the Indian agent.[310] He was expected to conduct agency business, erect buildings, supervise farming and mechanical operations such as the flour and sawmill, receive and distribute Indian supplies, manage the schools, accurately record accounts, care for livestock and correspond about necessary agency information. Further, it was noted that "these men take their families far into the wilderness, cut themselves off from civilization with its comforts and attractions, deprive their children of the advantages of education, live lives of anxiety and toil, give bonds for great sums of money, and be held responsible in some instances of hundreds of thousands of dollars a year, and subject themselves to ever ready suspicion."[311] It is no wonder competent men hesitated to accept the job or, after a short trial, resigned. Pay was less than a village postmaster or third-class clerk in Washington.[312] This was the case over the next few years when in rapid succession agents arrived at and departed the Absaroka Agency.

AGENT LEWIS H. CARPENTER

Agent Clapp was replaced with Lewis H. Carpenter, nominated on August 4, 1876, by President Ulysses S. Grant.[313] Evidently, the newly agent, a former Union army lieutenant, was a "man in moderate circumstances" and had difficulty coming up with a $40,000 bond required to hold office. On Carpenter's request, this was reduced to $10,000 and his funds posted on September 1, 1876.[314] Carpenter, thirty-nine years old, wasted no time departing from Syracuse, New York, with arrival at the Absaroka Agency on October 19. He officially took charge two days later.[315]

Calamity confronted the new agent when he reported to his superior in Washington of a November fire consuming the agency sawmill. He noted the building had been "considered unsafe" and the "engine and boiler condemned some time ago."[316] Carpenter aptly drew plans for a new proposed gristmill (wheat mill) and sawmill. They never came to fruition.[317] He disclosed further bad news to the commissioner of Indian affairs about the "severe"[318] winter the agency was experiencing. He relayed further there was no hay, and the freight wagons and horses "were unfit for use."[319] Added misfortune spread with news the Crow annuity supplies and food goods were stranded in Corrine, Utah. A suggestion for the Crow to self-sustain by hunting was not feasible due to lack of game from too much commotion by remaining troops and hostile Indians raids.[320] This triggered a state of "destitution" among the elder Crow, observed Carpenter, and "certain parties" quickly painted him as incompetent.[321] To ease tensions and perhaps to buy time until the wagon loads of goods arrived, the agent requested permission to purchase blankets, sugar, cloth and coffee from Bozeman's Gallatin Valley.[322] Subsequently, a large ad appeared in Bozeman's *Avant Courier* soliciting "Ten Thousand Pounds of 'C' Sugar and 6000 Pounds of Rio Coffee."[323]

An 1877 Crow census confirmed nearly 2,000 tribal members had left the agency to try to subsist by hunting, leaving about 780, the lowest number in years, in the vicinity of the agency.[324] Carpenter was optimistic that once "regular supplies" were obtained, the Crow could be induced to settle and remain close. Daily rations allotted during this period included per one hundred people 150 pounds of beef, 50 pounds of flour and corn, 10 pounds of pork, 3 pounds of beans, 8 pounds of sugar, 4 pounds of coffee and 1 pound each of tobacco, salt and soap.[325] However, annuities were months in the making; it was not until June 6 when Carpenter received notice of the goods shipping from Corinne, Utah.[326] Nine months into his job, Carpenter, perhaps with a sigh of relief, was replaced on July 13, 1877, by George W.

Frost, a former member of the Nebraska legislature and purchasing agent for the Union Pacific Railroad.[327]

AGENT GEORGE W. FROST

Considered an "accomplished business man" and a "clever and agreeable gentleman,"[328] Agent George Frost's first impressions of the Absaroka Agency would challenge both. He quickly discovered in his August debut "three rapid mountain torrents" must be crossed to even reach the site.[329] Next, scrutinizing the agency grounds, he noted there was a lack of adequate farmland and perceived the locale would have long, snow-covered winters and a short growing season. Nor was he pleased by the agency buildings "in a sadly neglected state," with adobe cracking and crumbling. Only a few were roofed.[330] Even the supplies, wagons, harnesses and teams he found marginal. He quickly discovered the agency lacked a functional sawmill. This is "an indispensable auxiliary," he moaned, for "I have no lumber to make coffins," let alone any means to make repairs.[331] The agent soon had more pressing concerns when "Indian scares" over rumors the Nez Perce, allies of the Crow and now fleeing from U.S. government troops, were going to make "the Agency their objective point."[332] Even though for years the Crow had been on good terms with the Nez Perce, for those fearful the tribes would join forces, Frost quickly reassured readers in the local newspaper there was no need for apprehension. The Crow are "perfectly loyal and friendly" to the whites.[333]

THE NEZ PERCE

Just two years prior to Frost's statement, in 1875, the Crow camped with Nez Perce warrior Looking Glass and about forty lodges on Pryor Creek, near present-day Huntley, Montana. The Sioux, Cheyenne and a few Arapahoe were attempting to steal the camp's horses. The Crow prepared for an attack. Plenty Coups remembered that day for his biographer Frank Linderman in 1928.

> We could not run, even had we wished to go…burdened as we were with our women, children, and horses.…There was nothing we could do but stand and fight.…Iron Bull and Sits-in-the-middle-of-the land were our chiefs.…"This is the day to go fighting to our Father," they told us. Those

Plenty Coups. *NAA INV 06631000.*

words sent my blood racing."…*The Nez Perce were not always friendly to us. There was sometimes war between us. But this time they were our friends, and always their warriors are brave men. If it had not been for them, we might have been badly whipped ourselves.*[334]

Since times had changed for the Nez Perce due to the steady influx of miners encroaching on Nez Perce lands, the U.S. government ordered the Nez Perce to relocate to a new reservation. Initially refusing to leave Oregon's Wallowa Valley, the three leaders—Joseph, Looking Glass and White Bird—agreed to the resettlement plan only when violent conflict became imminent in 1877.

Before the move, warriors from White Bird's band attacked and killed several white settlers. The U.S. Army retaliated against all Nez Perce. Fleeing to avoid defeat by the army, in early July 1877, Joseph, leader of the Wallowa band of the Nez Perce people, helped lead eight hundred Nez Perce with two thousand horses toward the Canadian border in a legendary 1,700-mile, three-and-a-half-month tactical retreat. They defeated the U.S. military in several battles throughout the summer with initial hopes of seeking refuge with the Crow. Fully aware the Nez Perce were wronged by white encroachments on their lands, the Crow feared the same could happen to them on their homelands. They were willing to sever their friendship with the Nez Perce for one with "their more powerful friends the whites."[335] It is also probable Crow leaders warned the people not to risk punishment and imprisonment by helping the Nez Perce.[336]

When the Nez Perce discovered the Crow were scouting and fighting with government troops, the strategy to join them was no longer an option, forcing Joseph and his band to head north to Canada.

Crow scouts were recruited at the Absaroka Agency in early September by General Samuel Sturgis and used as guards and barriers when the path of the Nez Perce crossed into present-day Yellowstone National Park. When the fleeing band entered the Clarks Fork Canyon and river, Crow scouts stole nearly one hundred horses from them, luring even more fellow tribesmen to join the troops in hope of gaining bounty for themselves.[337]

In rapid fashion, the Nez Perce followed down the Clarks Fork River to Canyon Creek, with the Crow and military on their heels. Just north of present-day Laurel, Montana, the Battle of Canyon Creek was fought on September 13, 1877. Crow participant Sits Down Spotted stated that the shooting was heavy at Canyon Creek.[338] However, in the face of fire, the Nez Perce successfully escaped, enabling them to reach the high plains opening to the northerly Big Snowy Mountains.

Sits Down Spotted. *Courtesy of author.*

Center is a scene from the Battle of Canyon Creek. *From* Harper's Weekly, *October 27, 1877.*

Given the depleted condition of the Nez Perce, low morale and loss of horses, the march was challenging. At this juncture, Crow oral history accounts relate attempts to aid the Nez Perce, including providing food and supplies and taking in Nez Perce women and children. The Crow also created diversions to lure the soldiers off the trail and pledged to the Nez Perce to shoot over one another's heads.[339]

On October 5, 1877, forty miles from their destination, the Nez Perce were encircled by U.S. troops. Exhausted and near starvation, Joseph told his people, "I am tired. My heart is sick and sad. From where the sun now stands I will fight no more forever."[340]

Crow Rights Are Threatened

Continuing complications plagued both Agent Frost and the Crow, namely, intruders on the reservation. Local stockmen created their own breed of unrest, often trailing cattle across prime hunting grounds on the Crow Reservation. Fees of one dollar per head were required to cross but often went unheeded, forcing the agent to threaten them with military removal.[341] With hopes of putting an end to such invasions, Blackfoot and other prominent tribesmen journeyed during early June 1878 to see Brigadier General Miles. They happened upon him near Fort Custer (approximately thirty miles east of Billings, Montana).[342]

Miles found the party of Crow "anxious" to get a message to the president, claiming "their rights have been disregarded and their reservation overrun."[343] Blackfoot acknowledged the Crow "have been given a good reservation…and want it for our home, [but] we want the Great Father to preserve it for us." Last but not least, the leader urged "that trespassers of all kinds, wolfers, trappers, prospectors and miners keep off our Reservation." During this meeting, Blackfoot presented a gun case as a gift to be given to President Hayes.[344]

Miles pleaded their case to his superior, recommending a favorable response would only be appropriate for the Crow who pledged "their loyalty—which has been maintained for seventy (70) years."[345] It is probable during this same visit the Crow invited Miles to a celebration in honor of their joint efforts with the military in removing the Sioux from the Yellowstone Valley. Reminiscing in his memoirs, Miles remained awestruck over the fine display of Crow clothing:

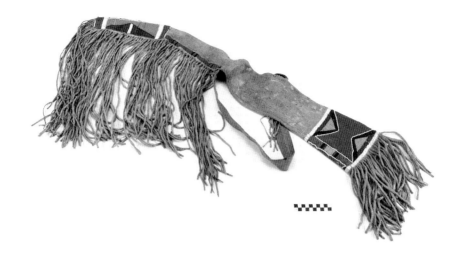

Gun case. *NMAI 203465catalog19/670.*

> *In all my experiences with Indians I have never seen such a display of decorations. The men were painted, and ornamented with the most brilliant feather-work. Their eagle headdress were waving in the air.... Their war jackets were bespangled with glittering pieces of flashing silver, elk teeth and mother of pearl, and one of the singular features of the display consisted in the fact that in the whole number there were no two Indians alike. They did not copy or duplicate, and all their work was of original design. The colors were the strongest and most durable character.... The eagle feathers, the porcupine work, the bear-claw necklaces, and the scalp locks of their enemies were evidence of their* [the Crows'] *wealth and prowess in war and the chase.*[346]

Evidently, Blackfoot's request on behalf of the Crow went unheeded. Within weeks, Miles was given orders to organize an August summer expedition to "establish a wagon route and telegraph line west of Fort Keogh" into the heart of the Yellowstone Valley, prime buffalo country.[347]

BANNOCK INDIANS ON THE MOVE

The Miles party, consisting of ten officers, one hundred soldiers, four civilians, five women and three children (including Miles's family), traveled "leisurely up the Yellowstone Valley," eventually setting up a camp near the former Crow agency of Fort Parker. Reverie was soon interrupted when a courier rode in bearing news: twenty-five lodges of Bannock Indians "who had gone on the warpath" were fleeing their Fort Hall, Idaho reservation and crossing into the park. This threat had potential to create "devastation" to the small settlements in their path.[348] Miles quickly sent his civilian guests to Fort Ellis and then departed with seventy-five men. Dividing them, forty were sent southerly to the Boulder River; the remaining thirty-five troops along with Miles traveled southeast toward the Clark Fork River to block hostiles' movement into the Yellowstone Valley.

His command gained an enlistment of seventy-five Crow scouts from the Absaroka Agency, causing us, recalled Miles, to appear "more like an Indian expedition."[349] Among the scouts was the French Canadian Rock Berthiaume (also spelled Bethunne), who was dispatched by Miles to access the Bannocks' strength.[350] Little Rock, as Berthiaume was also known, located the camp. He was subsequently discovered by the Bannack and taken as prisoner but then released. The scout then returned seventy-five miles to the Absaroka Agency armed with information but also with two Bannocks, who were probably emissaries. Immediately, Agent Frost put out guards to watch the Bannocks, while Little Rock reported to Miles.[351]

On September 5, 1878, near present-day Clark, Wyoming, troops surprised and engaged with the Bannock, killing eleven tribesmen and capturing thirty-one. Captain Andrew S. Bennett of the Fifth Infantry was killed, as were Little Rock and a second Crow scout, both found near Bennett. Rock left behind a widow and two children: Frank, five, and Josephine, three.[352]

6

ANNUITIES, INSPECTORS AND FRAUD

The Indian Goods Called Annuities

Mindful the Crow would need means of subsistence and clothing until results from farming could sustain them, Article 9 of the 1868 treaty stated the U.S. government was to provide for the Crow (and other Plains tribes) the following annuity articles to be disbursed for thirty years at their agency: to each male over fourteen years of age, "a suit of good substantial woolen clothing, consisting of a coat, hat, pantaloons, flannel shirt, and a pair of woolen socks." Each female over twelve would receive "a flannel skirt," or material to make it, "a pair of woolen hose, twelve yards of calico, and twelve yards of cotton domestics." For underage boys and girls were allotted flannel and cotton materials to sew a suit, "together with a pair of woolen hose for each." Food rations were also provided for four years amounting to one pound of meat and flour per day for every member over four residing on the reservation. A yearly census taken by the Indian agent provided estimated sums needed. Overseeing the distribution, an army officer would inspect and report on their quantity and quality.[353]

Wearing annuity goods at Fort Parker are Crow men photographed by William Henry Jackson in 1871. They include, left to right: Etcha-re-kash-cha-rach-a (Poor Elk), Kam-ne-but-see (Sits in the Middle of the Land or Blackfoot), A-pats-ke (Long Ears), I-sa-Seesh (He Shows His Face) and Mit-cho-ash (Old Onion). Little consultation with the Crow was sought on types of goods received. However, it was quickly found the issued pants and stockings were awkward and restraining to them, with recommendations they not be purchased again.[354] Likewise, the Crow found beaver traps of little consequence. The agent suggested heavy-duty kettles would be more beneficial.[355]

These disbursements became lively events, as witnessed by a visitor during the 1872 distribution at Fort Parker. "Soon the Indians began filing in through the gateway, and young and old of both sexes, ranged themselves on all sides of the court. Some were arrayed in well garnished robes, others in blankets of all colors and hues, some in full Indian costume, and all were possessed of comfortable apparel…not a poorly clad Indian in the entire assemblage." Prior to the distribution, Iron Bull urged the Crow to think of "things spiritual" and less of temporal goods. When the warehouse doors finally swung open, the observer noted employees came out "with their arms full" and in no time had a pile of goods. "Bolts of calico, sheeting and ticking, piles of tobacco, sacks of sugar, coffee and flour, kegs of powder, and other things unnumberable." At the close of this particular distribution, Bear Wolf, Pretty Eagle, their followers and four women, with blackened

Photographed by William Henry Jackson in 1871 and posed in front of Fort Parker are Crow men with annuity goods. *BAE GN 03418A.*

faces and carrying scalps, formed a circle. To the "beating of the drums… and…mournful chanting," they danced in a circle. Near the conclusion, "about thirty young Crows" rode in on captured Sioux horses, chanting of "their exploits…and glories." The day produced a "general satisfaction to all," and concluded with a horse race.[356]

Another traveler witnessed Nelson Story's ox train loaded "heavily with annuities" pulling into the Absaroka Agency in 1875.

> *A busy scene occurred; the Indians seated themselves in bands under their respective chiefs on the prairie, and awaited orders. Blackfoot, a prominent chief, was appointed by the other chiefs and headmen of the Mountain Crows, chief spokesman and orator of the day. He has the reputation of being the finest orator, and the ablest leader of the Crow Nation—is a very* [illegible] *and noble looking Indian, is very conspicuous and has great influence among his people,* [and] *has a powerful voice.*

The reporter noted it took two strenuous days with twelve men in wagons to disperse the goods. The Crow followed suit and appointed one of their own to distribute them. "They generally appeared to be well pleased," he added. In a show of gratitude, as was their custom, the chiefs presented buffalo robes to the agency heads.[357]

A census of the Crow taken by Agent Frost in 1877 estimated there were 3,281 Mountain and River Crow for whom he needed to purchase supplies.[358] A *Helena Weekly Herald* correspondent witnessed the distribution and stated the goods were the "largest" and "most satisfactory" in years. He observed the Crow appeared "warmly clad, fantastically ornamented, and in big cheer." Credit was given to Agent Frost for his judicious management.[359] The following year, journalist Fred M. Wilson provided added details of his visit and tour of the storeroom at the Absaroka Agency. Escorted "kindly" by Agent Frost, the guest found "staples of rice, sugar, flour, coffee, etc. which are regularly served out to the Indians.…These articles were of better quality than usually found on the table of an Eastern laboring man."[360] In the clothing ware rooms, Wilson saw equally impressing goods, "bale upon bale of blankets, red, blue, green and white in color. Ready-made clothing enough to start a wholesale supply store…woolen socks for the men. There were hats, boots, knives and forks, hunting knives, looking-glasses [binoculars] and tin cups and plates."[361]

Blue and red woolen flannel fabric was a practical distribution, being standard Crow dress of the time was sewn from the government-issued article. Often red flannel was used for fringed trimmings. The dress made in one piece, extended down a few inches above the ankles and adorned with elk teeth. Loose sleeves flowed to the elbow. Flannel leggings, all blue or blue with a red mixture, extended from ankles to mid-thigh.[362]

Another prevalent commodity distributed was sacked flour. It was freighted at "a considerable expense" with only small amounts consumed. Instead, the contents were emptied out, for the real prize was the flour sack:

Crow dress. *035B03F08.05 Bud Lake Coll. MHS.*

"its decorative colored printing was to an Indian woman a beautiful piece of material…or for hanging upon the interior wall of the lodge."[363] Oftentimes the sacks served as the binding edge on Crow dresses,[364] and then children became the unknown beneficiaries of the commodity. Their frustrated mothers, lacking proper pans and utensils, refused to bake—thus the sacked content was discarded. This became grand fun for the children to play in.[365] Bean rations contained in burlap sacks were treated similarly, with the sacks preferred over the content and used for household storage.[366]

Inspectors

Supplying Indian goods was a multimillion-dollar business. By the 1870s, it was considered "the chief arena for illegal and unjust economic gain at the expense of the government and the Indians."[367] Countless schemes were used to deprive the Indians and defraud the government ranging from selling inferior goods and inflating prices, to boosting transportation costs. Putting one's finger on the root of "Indian rings," a conspiratorial assembly of suppliers, businessmen and agency personal was difficult.[368]

Evidence of corruption in handling Indian affairs was long-standing.[369] In 1793, George Washington specifically requested laws for fraud prevention. An Episcopal minster writing in 1862 to the president condemned the ill character of Indian agents, government and contractor corruption, adding, "Tradition on the border says than an Indian agent with fifteen hundred dollars a year can retire upon an ample fortune in four years."[370]

To confront the endless ways to cheat and defraud, Congress established the Board of Indian Commissioners on April 10, 1869, "to correct mismanagement in the purchase and handling of Indian supplies."[371] The board comprised no more than ten men, hand-selected by the president, based on "intelligence and philanthropy," who served without pay.[372] The board worked diligently with "goodwill," dividing the country into divisions, with subcommittees assigned to tour agencies for better understanding.[373] More pragmatic was the board's determination to supervise and play an honest hand in procuring adequate and quality annuity goods.

The poor quality of goods distributed was confirmed by Blackfoot in 1873. "We get a pair of stockings, and when we put them on they go to pieces. They get some old shirts.…When we put them on, our elbows go right through them," and the tin kettles did not hold water. The blankets issued were also inferior as Blackfoot stated we "could blow through them."[374]

Another surety Congress passed on February 14, 1873, was the hiring of five inspectors (later reduced to three) who were to keep a vigilant eye on operations in the field and activities of the Indian agents. The inspectors were not a "panacea" but rather hoped an "instrument" for tighter management of the Indian service.[375] To bolster inspections and thwart unscrupulous dealings, it was recommended by 1875 for all Indian supplies and beef to undergo a three-point examination at "points of purchase," "shipment" and at the "agency."[376]

Despite the safeguards, an example of the ease of exploiting government coffers was provided by Tom Leforge. He explained that one winter while Agent Pease was away from Fort Parker, his nephew Zed Daniels became the acting agent. Daniels directed Leforge and others to cut logs for additional agency structures. Before heading out, the timber crew took liberty of the Crow goods, loading up "a big supply of provisions." Weekly forays were made for replenishments, with Daniels providing "all we asked for, and more." In the spring, the Leforge party returned to the agency, explained their logging operations to Agent Pease and then collected wages. Shortly afterward, an inspector accompanied Pease to assess the timber allegedly cut. Leforge knew what they would discover. "We had spent the whole winter in loafing, dancing, singing, drumming, and feasting," he stated. "Not a log had been cut!" Pease was said to have "raised a storm," but the matter was later dropped "as being but an amusing incident." Leforge and his gang were paid, and Pease had gotten away with hiring a relative. "Such loose and help-yourself business ways" chimed Leforge, "permeated the whole system of Indian management in those times."[377]

FRAUD

It has been said "there is no more malodorous chapter in the history of the frontier than that of dealings involving supplies for Indian Agencies."[378] As a result, it was the Indian who was the loser. To this end, in 1878 an investigation of fraud and corruption linked to Crow agency supply goods was led by Inspector Captain Edward Ball. Implicated were Montana pioneer and Gallatin Valley resident Nelson Story, former Crow agent Dexter Clapp and Agent George Frost.

Story had many connections to the Crow at the agency. He owned trading posts; hauled freight; and sold flour, hogs and cattle for beef distribution to the Crow. However, the charges against him claimed not all his business dealing with the agency were fair. In one instance he was accused of double-sacking flour freighted to the agency. This trick employed the use of two sacks. After the flour was examined and stamped by the inspector as acceptable, the top layer was stripped off to expose a second sack so it, too, could be stamped—thus doubling the agency inventory and profit to Story but shorting supplies for the Crow. When asked by an investigator how the Crow would subsist, Story replied, "There was plenty of buffalo" for them to survive on.[379] Also questionable and linked to Story was an inspection of

Fraud caricature of unscrupulous dealing in Indian supplies, torn blankets, empty rifle case and spoiled beef. *From* Frank Leslie's Illustrated Newspaper, *September 18, 1875.*

fifty-seven barrels of pork intended for agency use. Sold by Story, the pork proved not to be "mess pork," or meaty sides and shoulder, as required by the government, but the hogs' "entire head, shoulders, backbone, and tail."[380] The barrels were short the required 450 pounds, averaging about 250 pounds. Story was accused of trying to bribe Inspector Ball to ignore this, to no avail. Ball not only rejected the shipment of pork but then ascertained Agent Clapp was also a "party to the proposed fraud."[381] Further investigation reported by a second inspector, Colonel Edward C. Kemble, confirmed Ball's allegation that former Crow agent Clapp was aware of Story's misconduct.

Story's unscrupulous cattle practices were also at stake, leading to more accusations against Agent Clapp. Reportedly, with Clapp's permission, Story at one time illegally grazed 4,700 head of cattle and 1,000 head of horses on the Crow Reservation. In exchange, Story was to provide hay and grain to agency parties traveling through.[382] Another cattle scheme involved altering the agency "ID" brand to reflect different ownership. Additionally, cattle weights were manipulated so only Story's heaviest steers were weighed and sold, using this average to determine the total amount the government paid him per pound. In short, the government paid for unaccounted poundage while the Crow were getting less beef supplies.[383] Despite Ball's report of these misdeeds, two grand juries and an Indian Commission investigation failed to establish any wrongdoings against Story.[384]

Ten months after Agent Frost complained to the commissioner of Indian affairs about Story's cattle trespassing, Frost himself was replaced for allegations he paid for goods not delivered, his failure to pay employees and payment to nonexistent employees.[385]

His successor, David Kern, arrived at the post in late September 1878, eager to do the job he was hired to do. Kern heard less than encouraging words about the agency from Frost, and two weeks into the job, without pay, Kern was told it would be three weeks until matters over a beef contract disagreement between the agency and the government could be settled. For this dispute and "other potent reasons," Kern resigned.[386] J. Rainsford was acting agent until a new agent was nominated.[387]

7

AGENT AUGUSTUS KELLER

Replacing acting agent J. Rainsford was Augustus Ruffner Keller. He was the son of Daniel and Susannah Keller, born in Ohio on July 1, 1838. His boyhood days were spent on the family farm. As he reached manhood, he began studying law but was interrupted by the civil unrest in the country and at age of twenty-four enlisted in the Ninetieth Ohio Regiment. He made rank of captain for Company I and later quartermaster on the staff of General Stedman. On his return to civilian life, he again took to farming but was also active in politics, serving as chairman on the local Republican Central Committee. He then came to the attention of Ohio governor Rutherford Hayes, who appointed him to the Board of Trustees for the Ohio Penitentiary and later as agent to the Crow.

A.R. Keller's westward travel to the Absaroka Agency may have been an omen for the challenges he would face as agent. Departing Ohio, he arrived at the rail terminus in Black Rock, Utah. Here, he boarded a stagecoach bound for the 250-mile trip to Bozeman. The town was struck by "severe snow storm" that hindered his departure for two days, but at last for the final leg of the journey Keller managed to hire an "overcrowded open conveyance." After 200 miserable miles over the "summit of the mountain" in subzero weather, the new agent arrived at the Absaroka Agency on December 22, 1878.[388]

The following day, he took "formal possession" of agency property, including the adobe buildings, which he noted were crumbling and "in very bad condition." He also came at a time of great unrest for the Crow peoples amid reports from settlers of stolen mules, cattle and petty thefts by his newfound charges. Keller's ten-page letter to his superior spelled out further disappointments. Present farming operations were "inconsequential," for there had been "no effort" to teach the Crow to farm. Nor did he discover any attempt for suppression of trespassers on the Crow Reservation, casting a "general feeling here that the reservation is a public goose that everyone has a right to pick." The school "amounts to but little except in name," he scoffed. Even the "Home" was "a farce," but Keller pledged his "undivided strength, muscle, mind and heart to the work."[389]

His will was promptly put to the test by several issues looming larger than the deteriorating agency: unresolved issues with trespassers—namely, the cattlemen and miners—and then the pressing need for the Crow to learn farming practices.

Keller quickly found himself on the wrong side of the cattlemen, "a strong body in this country," he quipped. Their continued trespasses on the Crow Reservation agitated the Crow,[390] and the intruders became even a stronger presence by their efforts to gain rights to trail herds across the reservation. The astute cattlemen knew trailing through the reservation from the Wyoming-Nebraska line was the shortest route to eastern markets, cutting off nearly four hundred miles and thus creating a substantial savings.[391] Confounding the matter were the herds of cattle already grazing on the reservation belonging to several white men married to Crow women. Many of the cattle had a brand similar to the agency's "ID" brand, creating a challenge to distinguish ownership. Keller was certain over the past two years some five hundred government cattle had been stolen. However, he was given warning by "leading citizens" when neighboring cattle drifted on the reservation "to take no notice."[392]

Bearded, Agent Augustus Rufus Keller (*center*) is posed with his employees at the Absaroka Agency in 1881. An adobe structure frames them. Children seated on the ground are unidentified. Seated front row, far left, Alex Hundley, two unidentified men, Agent Keller, possibly Mrs. Maggie Keller, possibly Mrs. Norton and far right, William H. Norton, whose home still stands in Columbus, Montana. Standing immediately behind the seated individuals, left to right, are three unknown men, Barney Bravo, Horace Countryman, Addison Quivey, Hugh Campbell and Tom Kent. Standing, back row, centered between two unknown men, is Tom Shane. Yearly wages (1880) were as follows: clerk and physician, $1,200; farmer, carpenter, herder, $840; blacksmith, $800; teacher, $720; engineer, miller, second blacksmith, $600; interpreter, $400; matron, $360; irregular laborers, $500.

This is one of several period images taken by noted frontier photographer F.J. Haynes: Agent Keller and employees. *H-4064 Haynes Coll. MHS.*

COUNCIL MEETINGS

Mounting tension prompted a series of council meetings between Keller and Crow leaders held at the Absaroka Agency on March 8, April 23 and May 16, 1879. Speaking at the first meeting, Blackfoot and Horse Guard opposed "white men running across this reservation, settling upon it and driving cattle across it." When the leaders were done talking, all the Crow stood up as a show of support.[393] A second meeting affirmed the Crow did not want the cattle eating their grass, frightening buffalo or their ponies straying off with the strangers. Blackfoot in a "forcible manner unbraided his people" for not being proactive in notifying the agent of further intrusions. Then turning to Keller, he pleaded, "I ask you to hold my country for me and to let no one travel through it. It will make my heart feel good."[394] "It will only hurt the Crows to have a cattle trail across their land,"commented Bull Goes Hunting "[and next] they will build houses."[395] "We all have one heart about the whites coming on our reservation," exclaimed Two Belly.[396]

At the May 16 meeting, even when faced with a permit from a cattle drover to cross their land, the Crow were unyielding. Iron Bull insisted, "I have told the Agent once what was in my heart. I have the same mind today. I don't want any cattle driven across my Reservation." "I am an old man but

I will talk for my children," stated White Forehead. "I hope the Great Father won't let them come over our land with their cattle. By and by they will come and stay on the Reservation. It is good land and the white men want some of it."[397] This same sentiment was echoed by Big Ox, who spoke for the River Crow. "We have always been friendly with the white men and we always will be, but we don't want them to make a cattle trail across the Reservation. We have told you (the Agent) so. Every time you asked us about it. We have not two hearts. There are lots of us, but we have one mind."[398]

Farming

Keller was fully cognizant farming instruction was mandatory under the 1868 treaty. But with wild game becoming increasingly scarce, he realized it must become a priority for future sustainment of the Crow. The meetings served a platform to promote and encourage the Crow do so. Farming, he pointed out in the council of March 8, 1879, had "many advantages over their present nomadic manner of living."[399] It would provide food when game became scarce. Seeing the wisdom in this, Iron Bull agreed. "I think the Agent has much sense. I want to ask him so much about things. We don't know what we are doing, the Agent talks right. If I wait till the Buffalo are all gone before I learn to work[,] I'll be poor. I want you to show me how to work, and I want you to ask the Great Father to give me things to work with."[400] Blackfoot, the principal speaker at both Fort Laramie and the Judith Basin negotiations, addressed his people:

> *I want you to listen to me and understand what I say. I try to do the best I can for you. You must behave yourselves always. If your Chiefs were fools, you would all be fools.…The white man want[s] to do you good, they tell you about farming, think of that.…I have always thought of farming. I have planted tobacco every spring since a boy. If we farm[,] we won't be poor.…If some farm this spring, and some more next spring, that[']s good.*[401]

Old Crow, with conflicted feelings, commented, "We are all going to farming. We want to live right here." He also planned to continue hunting, but when it turned "stormy and cold" he'd return to the agency. "I have two hearts about it," he concluded.[402] Plenty Coups also struggled: "We like to live in a Lodge [tipi] you build us a house [as incentive to farm], we like that too. We want both."[403]

Blackfoot would not live to see the vast changes he encouraged for the Crow people. His death notice was brought to the Absaroka Agency on July 3, 1879. Agent Keller forwarded the news to Commissioner of Indian Affairs Ezra A. Hoyt as follows:

> *A messenger just in from camp located at the foot of Heart Mountain, some distance this side of Stinking water River—distance about seventy five miles from the Agency brings word that the distinguished Crow Chief Blackfoot is dead. He had by far greater abilty* [sic] *than any man of his tribe. He was possessed of a fine physique, was a natural orator and was always a firm friend of the white race. His last request was to have his remains brought to the Agency and deposited with his kindred.*[404]

Despite the loss of this great leader, Keller kept encouraging the Crow to farm and was pleased by what he was hearing from them. The confident agent boasted to his superior, "I can have a nation of Farmers organized of these Crows, within a few years."[405] As added motivation, new houses were offered for those who did so.[406] Despite Keller's optimism, statistics from this period show only forty-one acres had been cultivated. What is clear, the Crow were yet actively hunting, trapping and trading. Records for 1880 show a sale proceed for their robes and furs totaling $27,750, suggesting there was little incentive to give up their present lifestyle.[407] This along with other factors motivated the U.S. government to instruct Keller to hold another council meeting with them.

Crow leaders posed intently in front of an adobe building at the Absaroka Agency. Medicine Crow, seated left, was born in 1848 and became a renowned Crow warrior with twenty-two war deeds to his credit.[408]

Near the time of this photograph, circa 1881, it was noted his hands were blistered and scarred, not from skirmishing with enemy tribes or marred from a recent hunt, but from tilling and farming the land behind a walking plow or hoe. His conduct was encouraging and viewed as a great step toward progress for those responsible for administering Indian policy.[409]

White Temple, seated center, more commonly called Iron Bull, was also among the first to implement the U.S. government policy aimed at providing self-sufficiency through an agricultural lifestyle. Others identified include, seated right, Bird In Ground, and standing left to right, Sits Before a Cloud and Yellow Fringe, also identified as Stands Before the Cloud.

Council meetings often served dual purposes and dual agendas, and the March 23, 1880 assembly at the Absaroka Agency was no exception. Keller first addressed the Crow, "Many of you have at various times expressed a determination to engage in farming, and the time has now approached for you to make a vigorous effort to settle upon your land, and commence a new manner of life. You cannot do it by talking, you must act."[410]

Replacing the now-deceased Blackfoot as principal leader was Iron Bull, who supported the shift to farming. This man of significance had two hundred members in his band.[411]

> *Last spring everyone in the room said that they wanted to farm. I belong to you and I have told you many times. We do not know how to commence farming, but we are all willing to try. We can't do much at first, we know that but we can all do a little and we want to commence now and build a house to live in, so that we will not be cold when the snows come.*[412]

Horse Guard voiced, "There are a lot of us that want to farm. Some of us can commence this spring and some next spring. It won't be long before

Crow in front of agency building. *H-553 Haynes Coll. MHS.*

we all have a house and some cattle and chickens and we will always have plenty to eat and can keep warm in the winter."[413]

Plenty Coups, a fearless warrior with significant spiritual success, also spoke. In his early twenties, the chief had two visions revealing he should cooperate with approaching white peoples. A tiny chickadee that survived a windstorm revealed to him his first vision: "It is a mind that leads to power."[414] The second vision indicated cattle would soon replace the buffalo.

CHIEF "HORSE-GUARD."

Horse Guard. *From* Frank Leslie's Illustrated Newspaper, *November 26, 1887.*

Near the time of this conference, the great herds were diminishing, thus leading Plenty Coups to act on his visions. In the spirit of cooperation, he humbly stated, "I have a heart and thought I had a mind, but the white men think for me, what I want to do, I don't do very much, I do what the white men want me to do."[415]

Crow band member The Spaniard announced, "We are all ready" to farm. Others agreeing were Crazy Head, Shot in the Jaw, Bull Nose, Spotted Horse, Young Bird, Horse Guard and Old Crow.[416]

MINING ISSUES

For years, increased trespassers and mining activity on the reservation were concerns. Keller was aware the mining settlement of Emigrant Gulch, near the western mountainous portion of the Crow Reservation, was steadily growing.[417] Additional mining operations along the eastern fringe of the reservation on the headwaters of the Clarks Fork River also agitated the Crow, who wanted them removed.[418]

Their multiple requests prompted Keller to lend his support and thus serve "notice to all trespassers that these irregularities must cease."[419] The agent was also fearful an upsurge in mining activity would spawn a "stampede" of miners onto the reservation with potential for heightened trouble.[420] Pressures and demand for the Crow to sell this region prompted Keller to shift the tone of the council meeting.[421]

"A part of your Reservation contains mines and the Great Father feels that it might be better for you to dispose of that part of your land," began Keller,

"You never go there, and it is of but little use to you."[422] This news alarmed the Crow" "I never heard you say anything before [about selling the land]," responded The Spaniard.[423] Keller quickly added President Rutherford B. Hayes requested six Crow leaders travel as soon as possible to discuss the matter in Washington, D.C.

Crazy Head suggested the Great Father should come to them for the discussion.[424] According to Plenty Coups, he was the first chosen delegate. He asked Two Belly, the senior River Crow, to join him. Four more members were selected by Keller: Medicine Crow, twenty-nine years old and a highly noted war leader; Pretty Eagle, also an accomplished warrior in his mid-thirties; Long Elk, a noted band leader; and Old Crow, the senior delegate, in his mid-forties, and a respected band leader.[425] Several members of Long Elk's band were married to white traders and agency employees, and he was concerned the government would take the land "without paying for it."[426]

Crow Delegation to Washington, D.C.

Three days later, March 26, 1880, Keller and the six Crow leaders departed for Washington, D.C.[427] Such visits were used as much to impress upon the Indians the wealth and power of the of the white nation as they were for negotiations. Even before their arrival, Washington's *Evening Star* announced the Crow were on their way to confer about "certain lands in their reservation" the settlers coveted. The paper postulated, "It is thought that the Crows will agree to cede the land to the government."[428]

Travel to Washington was no easy affair. Plenty Coups later reminisced,

> *It was during the Spring. There was no railroad yet in our county, and we had to travel by stagecoach which carried a light at night. We traveled in two coaches…set out* [leaving] *from the old agency* [Fort Parker].… *We traveled toward Butte* [Montana], *which took us four nights and five days.…At Butte, we rested for the first time. We slept a whole day and night. And I combed my hair for the first time since leaving our camp. Early the next morning we were told to dress quickly and eat.…The teams were ready and we traveled down the mountain.*[429]

That evening the Crow encountered members of the Bannock tribe and heard stories about the "fast wagon" (train), "a big black horse with his belly nearly touching the ground. This horse had a big bell on his back. He ran so fast that every time he stopped, he puffed."[430] Two days later, the Crow boarded a fast wagon in Ogden, Utah, recalled Plenty Coup.

> *We placed our bundles on shelves and looked out of the window. The train followed the river. Through the window we could see many horses, game, and mountains....We thought the journey was grand. I realized, however, that it was not a horse that pulled it* [the train] *and I wondered what made it go so fast.*[431]

During a brief stopover in Chicago, Plenty Coup witnessed ice breaking up on Lake Michigan, and it was also "the first time I had seen so many white people together."[432] Boarding another train, they finally arrived in Washington at the Baltimore and Potomac rail station. The following morning, the Crow met with President Hayes.[433]

The 1880 Crow delegation to Washington included sitting, left to right: Old Crow, Medicine Crow, Long Elk, Plenty Coups and Pretty Eagle; standing left to right: interpreter Addison M. Quivey, Two Belly, Agent Augustus Keller and Tom Stewart, also an interpreter. For over a month, they were in Washington, D.C., speaking with President Hayes as well as

The 1880 Crow Delegation. *MOB.*

Pretty Eagle. *NAA INV.06635000.*

touring the city, the Capitol and Mount Vernon. President Hayes discussed his goals for the Crow to become skilled as farmers and the importance of educating their children. He also informed them a railroad was going to be built through the Yellowstone Valley. However, his principal concern was to convince them to sell the portion of their reservation containing the mines. Pretty Eagle later related that the president "wanted from the Boulder to the Mountains and all the mountains, and a road cut through our land to drive cattle over, and a Railroad to run through our land. The whites got together and talked until it made my heart feel dead."[434]

Newspaper reporters were fascinated by the physical appearance of the Crow, claiming them as the "finest specimens of the race yet seen in Washington....Each wears a magnificent war shirt of buckskin, finely embordered, beaded and adorned with many white weasel tails."[435] The ermine or weasel tails attached represented a captured gun, a horse or a coup proper.[436] "They are a fine looking set of Indians. Their faces are very good," observed another reporter.[437]

The Crow, Bannock and Shoshone tribal members, also visiting at the time, were treated to a social event with Washington dignitaries in the Tremont House.[438] However, it was reported the "most interesting feature of the evening" was the conversation in sign language between Old Crow and Tendoy of the Bannock Tribe.[439]

During negotiations, the delegates refused to sell lands east of the Clarks Fork River; nor did they yield to government pressure for a railroad, telegraph line or cattle trailing over their reservation. According to Pretty Eagle, the disgruntled president told the delegates that "if we did not give it [the land] up it might be bad for us, that they might put us [the Crow] some other place."[440]

In an effort to yet sway the Crow into a favorable agreement, the delegates were given $20 (about $540 today) spending allowance as well as tours of the city, including to Mount Vernon. This prolonged their stay. "We were in Washington a long time, recalled Plenty Coups. I became anxious to return home."[441] Evidently, the tactic worked. The weary delegation did submit to a provisional agreement with the U.S. government. They also pledged to promote and encourage adoption of the agreement to their fellow tribesmen waiting at home. "Although we dreaded the long journey home, we were glad."[442]

Encouraged by Charles Barstow, the Crow, as well tribes visiting the Absaroka Agency, were taught to sketch. Known as ledger drawings, the images shed light on significant events dating from 1879 to 1884. Memorable

Top: Ledger Drawing. *1930.19 Barstow Collection, MSUB Special Collections.*

Bottom: Ledger Drawing. *1930-27 Barstow Collection, MSUB Special Collections.*

and sketched by Medicine Crow were monitors on the Potomac River and animals he observed at the zoo while a delegation member in Washington.

Charles Barstow in Charge

In the absence of Agent Keller in Washington, D.C., acting agent Charles H. Barstow had his hands full at the agency. Keller's instructions were to retain the Crow near the agency until the return of the delegation.[443] For the Crow, who often supplemented their diet with wild meat, remaining at the agency meant less hunting success, as game was getting scarce. For Barstow, it meant providing them with more beef and food rations.

This proved to be a challenge. "I need the cattle badly," Barstow stated in a desperate message carried by a special courier to cattleman and agency employee Tom Kent.[444] Further needs were exposed to prominent Bozeman rancher and contractor Nelson Story, "I must have the cattle" (emphasis in original).[445]

In attempts to prolong meat supplies, Barstow reduced beef rations by half, causing the hungry Crow to become "clamorous."[446] He succeeded in acquiring a portion of the needed supply of cattle in time for the arrival of the returning Crow delegates.[447] Barstow perceived that if the Crow were hungry during their pending council meeting, they would be in "no mood" to favorably consider the sale of a portion of their reservation.[448]

The acting agent also had other agency concerns. Scarlet fever, contracted the previous spring from visiting Shoshone and Bannock Indians, was now afflicting the Crow. The sickness caused frequent moving of the camps. Treatment by agency physician Dr. J.H. Willard was considered "skillful" but could not prevent the deaths of forty-three Crow.[449]

In a letter dated April 1, 1880, Barstow, however, communicated a bit of positive news to Keller, yet in Washington. Crow leaders Iron Bull, Bull Goes Hunting and a brother to Blackfoot had found desirable farm ground two miles north of the Absaroka Agency. "They are the first Crows to undertake an agricultural life and much depends on them being satisfied with their change," remarked Barstow.[450] He added he would "encourage them in every possible way.[451]

Barstow was impatiently waiting for Keller and the Crow to return; "I have been expecting you every day,"[452] he wrote the last day of May. The horse teams were ready to convey them from the Stillwater River and homeward to the Absaroka Agency.[453] Within days of their arrival at the agency, a tribal council was held to discuss the provisional document with the rest of the Crow people.

A Pivotal Meeting

"This is an important occasion," opened Agent Keller at the June 12, 1880 council. "Much of your comfort during future years depends upon your actions today. You sent your chiefs a long distance from their home to meet the Great Father.…They have now returned to tell you what was done."[454] Continuing, the agent read the entire proposed agreement, stopping to point out boundaries on a map. Keller encouraged the Crow to accept the agreement, trusting proceeds from the land sale would permit purchases of livestock and farming equipment to ease their farming transition. Taking the floor, influential leader Iron Bull spoke out adamantly against the provisional settlement.

> *I was willing to have the Reservation cut off from the Boulder, but now they want to have the country east of Clarkes Fork (Clarks Fork River). I wanted to go to that country to live, but none of you would go with me. I want you all to listen to me. We have never got any pay for the gold that has been already taken from our land.*[455]

Refusing to sell lands east of the Clarks Fork (of the Yellowstone River), Iron Bull pointed to the map and penciled in the boundary, "This is the amount of country I am willing to sell, and it is all that I will give my consent to sell." His devised plan would allow mining areas west of the Clarks Fork to be sold but not east of it. A great deal of trust was placed in Iron Bull, for "every Indian in the house arose" and "very cheerfully" signed the amended pact.[456]

Payments ceding the 1.6 million acres to the government amounted to $750,000 over a twenty-five-year period. In addition, the agreement provided each of head of family an allotment of 320 acres, one-half to be farmland, the rest suitable for grazing. The rest of the Crow members were to be allotted 160 acres in the same proportion. The agreement was ratified on April 11, 1882.[457]

THE NORTHERN PACIFIC RAILWAY COUNCILS

In the spring of 1879, the Northern Pacific Railway prepared to push west from Bismarck, Dakota Territory, where, due to bankruptcy, westward progress had stalled for five years.[458] By 1880, surveyors had begun progressing into the Yellowstone Valley and onto the Crow Reservation. Upon entering the reservation, they encountered Spotted Horse and a group of young Crow warriors who told them to leave, threatening to pull out their survey stakes.[459]

Even though the 1868 treaty protected Crow lands from all disturbances, including railroad expansion, a flurry of letters regarding surveying rights resulted. Secretary of the Interior Carl Schurz dispatched a message to Agent Keller. "No Rail Road Company," he stated "has any right to make surveys on the Crow Reservation without the consent of the Indians."[460] This was disregarded by railroad surveyors, who continued to encroach on Crow lands another thirty miles.[461] Namesake of present-day Billings, Montana, Fredrick Billings, president of the Northern Pacific Railroad, then instructed his men to suspend surveys on the Crow Reservation south of the Yellowstone River until agreeable measures were made with the Crow.[462]

A government administration change on March 8, 1881, brought to office a new secretary of the interior, Samuel J. Kirkwood, replacing Schurz. Kirkwood viewed things differently than his predecessor, believing the Northern Pacific had the right to enter the reservation for preliminary surveys. The ambiguity between Crow treaty rights versus railroad privileges led to three council meetings in 1881 with the Crow and government officials.[463]

Astride his horse is Poor Elk (Thin Elk), one of eleven Crow who signed the Fort Laramie Treaty of 1868 with the US. government. Nearby, lodges fan along the creek while picketed ponies patiently wait. In the same vicinity, a direct product of the treaty is the Crow's second agency, the Absaroka Agency. Standing left to right are Crazy Pend d'Oreille; Sacred Mountain Sheep, wife of Medicine Crow, holding their daughter; Medicine Crow; Big Shoulder Blade; and unidentified. Seated left to right are Crane in the Sky; Hoop on the Forehead; Bird in Ground; and unidentified. Many of these leaders participated in the railroad councils.

Halting their buffalo hunt, forty chiefs and head men appeared for the first council on May 26, 1881, at the Absaroka Agency. The listed included Iron Bull, Old Onion, Takes Wrinkle, Long Hair, Spotted Horse, Bear Wolf, Pretty Eagle, Old Guts, Stiff Penis, Bear in the Water, Black Hawk,

Crow group with tipi. *H-551 Haynes Coll. MHS.*

Medicine Crow, the Fringe, Old Dog, Crazy Sister in Law, Bull All the Time, Bad Snow, Crane in the Sky and Good Hearted Old Woman.[464]

Brother Van Orsdel opened the council with a prayer. Agent Keller next read messages to the Crow from the commissioner of Indian affairs and secretary of state. After the correspondence was "carefully" interpreted, Keller encouraged the Crow to speak "freely" about the pending railroad before sending their response to the Great Father."[465]

Both Old Onion and Iron Bull expressed the need to think about the matter. "We all ought to talk it over, one with another first," stated the latter. The well-seasoned Washington delegate, Medicine Crow, reasoned, "I know what a Railroad is. If we say yes, the whites will bring the Railroad across our land and it will be good. If we say no, the whites will bring it just the same. We had better say yes."[466]

Once the railroad discussion ended, the Crow deferred to other topics, in particular, their willingness to farm and the demand for more houses. Crane in the Sky said, "I want you to write this down and send it to the Great Father. I am not poor, but I want to go to work and build a house. There are Indians here who don't talk much, but they want houses and farms." He listed them as "Old Guts, Black Hawk, Two Bears, Scrapes a Robe, Man that Lives in a Cloud, and Throws an Enemy's Lodge Open."[467]

A second council on June 18, 1881, was held with Fellows D. Pease, right-of-way agent for the Northern Pacific Railroad. Matters of rail construction, establishment of depots and train stations were discussed and interpreted for the Crow by Tom Stuart. After a stated full understanding, 107 Crow, including Big Medicine, signed their consent for rail construction through the reservation to begin. Although payment was not discussed, this was not to "impede the progress."[468]

The last assembly gathered August 22, 1881, at the Absaroka Agency. At stake was the payment amount for the ceded right-of-way lands. Opening details were provided by spectator Joseph Kern. "Garbed in full regalia of war paint and feathers, the chiefs and a retinue of 30 or 40 appeared on the skyline of the ridge just west of the agency buildings. Here they paused, giving the group gathered at the agency a full view of their grandeur and then swept down the bluffs and into the Agency enclosure."[469] The Northern Pacific Railroad contingency was represented by former Crow Indian agent Fellows Pease, right-of-way mediator. Others included Llewellyn A. Luce, assistant attorney general, Office of Indian Affairs; William H. Walker, General Land Office; Charles A. Maxwell, Office of Indian Affairs; Wilbur Fisk Sanders and I.H. Pierce, attorneys for the

Big Medicine Man. *H-949 Haynes Coll. MHS.*

Northern Pacific; and J.T. Dodge, railroad engineer of the Northern Pacific Railroad.[470]

The council was opened by Judge Luce's explanation of the Railroad Act of 1864 and the Treaty of 1868. Next he displayed a map of the Crow Reservation showing the rail tracks. He clarified that the railroad needed a four-hundred-foot-wide right-of-way though the reservation, plus additional ground for rail depots and machine shops.[471]

Both Crazy Head and Two Belly spoke in favor of the railroad. Others worried about the possible loss of timber, including Spotted Horse, who less than a year ago confronted a survey party, threatening to pull out their survey stakes. At the council he "drew his knife and wanted the commissioners and agent to pledge that no timber should be cut."[472]

On the issue of payment, Agent Keller thought $22,000 was sufficient; Enemy Hunter wanted $400 for each lodge. Plenty Coups, the thirty-two-year-old warrior, brought the matter to a closure. "I will touch the pen and sign for all the Crow if you pay us $30,000." When Luce countered $25,000, the matter was settled and the agreement signed first by Plenty Coups followed by Thin Belly and 278 further chiefs and heads of families.[473] The agreement was ratified by Congress on April 11, 1882, ceding 1.5 million acres and a 400-foot right-of-way, an additional 5,650.7 acres from the Crow for the railroad.[474]

The Crow and Agent Keller did plenty of negotiating in 1881, but the demands on his charges were not done yet. On July 5, 1881, a meeting was held to gain Crow perspective on allowing the Northern Cheyenne band of Little Wolf to live on their reservation. This was an attempt by the government to consolidate some of the reservations. It was explained the Cheyenne would not own any of the land but merely reside there. The Crow responded that the Cheyenne were welcome to visit, but they declined to let them live jointly on the reservation.[475]

Spotted Horse. *B-491, Denver Public Library.*

THE COWBOYS

Keller was also juggling other troubling issues when north of the Yellowstone River cowboys killed a Crow who was attempting to return a stray horse to the reservation. With bravado, the cowboys threatened to kill "on sight" any additional Crow found on their cattle range. "It is deemed no crime to kill an Indian, but rather an act of heroism," Keller cynically wrote to his superior.[476]

The issue filtered down to Secretary of the Interior Samuel Kirkwood, who perceived any rustling and plundering of cattle was naturally "thrown" on the Indian. He mused, he had no doubt, "lawless white men roaming through this country [had] committed" the crimes. Given the cattlemen's "temper and state of mind," a government inspector dispatched to look into the matter was warned to try hard to prevent an "outbreak" between the cowboys and the Crow.[477] Likewise, Keller sternly advised the Crow "to stay clear of the cattlemen." He cautioned the "Great Father" might be on friendly terms with them now but that could change if they failed to heed his instructions.[478]

FALL HARVEST AND FAREWELL

One great source of accomplishment and pride for Keller was his witness of the 1881 crop harvest at the agency. Proven efforts were demonstrated by Iron Bull, Bull Goes Hunting, The Fringe, Medicine Crow, Thin Belly, Bear in Water, Dog Eye, Bull All the Time, Old Alligator, Little Antelope, The Sharing, Crane in the Sky, Sitting Weasel, Child in the Mouth, Fire Fish, Spotted Buffalo, Little Face, Charges Strong, Plenty Wings, Dummy, Milo Seketer and Fire Bear. The agent proudly noted their "first combined systematic effort" was revealed in the harvest of 30,000 pounds of potatoes, 12,000 pounds of turnips, 3,000 pounds of beets and 1,000 pounds each of onions and carrots and 300 heads of cabbage. Seeds taken to the root cellar for next year's planting he viewed as "collaborative evidence" of their desire to continue to farm.[479] However, before he could see the results, Keller resigned, departing to his family and homeland in Ohio.

8

AGENT HENRY J. ARMSTRONG

The new year of 1882 brought another change to the Crow with Henry J. Armstrong replacing Augustus Keller as agent. Challenging battles of another sort soon awaited this former army captain from Kansas. In his first report, he wrote, "I believe I assume charge of this agency at a time that may be said to be the crisis in the history of the Crows."[480] The Crows were not yet proficient as farmers, and the wild game they were dependent on was "almost gone."[481] With this means diminishing, Armstrong warned the Crow must learn farming practices to survive but recognized they "cannot change the nature to which they were created in a day." They must be "handled very carefully," he added.[482] The agent began "laying plans for the future" but first needed to convince his superiors in Washington, D.C.[483]

Settling the Crow "permanently" on their best farm ground seemed the logical choice. "These little creek bottoms that surround this agency are entirely inadequate," Armstrong lamented to the commissioner of Indian affairs, and would not provide enough future farm land for them. On the other hand, the agent understood the valley of the Big Horn, along the eastern fringe of the Crow Reservation, contained "the most extensive" and "best soil." It was also favored by the Crow.[484] He confessed, "My heart is down on the ground—as the Crows say when I think of the future of these people…confined to this locality which is the most unfavorable part of their country."[485]

Armstrong took up the crusade for their relocation, although he didn't want to "annoy" or "trouble"[486] the commissioner or "presume too much."

He believed it crucial the Crow resettle in their best territory, rationalizing, "every dollar spent here makes it more difficult to remove the agency."[487] He concluded, "I dread the task" and the increased responsibility but considered it a "necessity."[488]

The path of the Crow was obvious in Armstrong's response to Little Whetstone, who confided "he had two hearts. One told him to go and hunt buffalo, and the other told him to stay and farm." The agent insisted he stay to farm,[489] believing this was the mode of "life which they must adopt sooner or later or become extinct."[490]

"Jottings of a Wanderer," a news column written in 1882 by the traveler "F.M.W.," illustrates the extent of Agent Armstrong's efforts to teach them farming methods. The "wild region" had undergone change, for "many" of the Crow selected homesteads and "preparing to open up farms." At the Absaroka Agency itself was a one-hundred-acre cultivated field "divided into 3-acre plots and allotted" for those willing to work. Although vegetables of "all kinds" were planted in the agency field, potatoes were the "principal crop."[491] The process, remarked Armstrong, was "exceedingly vexatious." One of the first lessons for the Crow was how to properly harness a horse, followed by techniques to hook up the plow and usage of the implement.[492]

Armstrong's eventual pleadings drew the attention of Secretary of the Interior Henry Teller, who sensed the issue of relocating the Crow could create protest as well as require new legislation. It was suggested the agent gain consent from local whites and the Crow before proceeding further with the relocation.[493] This prompted Armstrong to hold a December 1882 council with the Crow. "The Indians were divided"—one faction "favorable to the proposition to select the best part of the country" was under the influence of Thin Belly. He "knew the Little Horn country was better" because it was "not so rocky." Another faction, fearing their reservation might be reduced by another land sale, "does not want the agency removed," reported Armstrong. Instead, this party under Plenty Coups and Pretty Eagle wanted the Crow to "take up and hold all the valleys on their reservation." A third party under Bear Wolf, "thoroughly wild," opposed any action. Spotted Horse, "one of the wildest," claimed he would move to the Little Horn "whether the government liked him over there or not."[494]

The Crow and Armstrong were also battling other elements beyond their control. The "severely cold" winter of 1883 coincided with the time of declining buffalo herds, both of which created hunting challenges. Reports described some bands of Crow hunters were "moderately successful in taking elk and deer" while others were "suffering with hunger." Armstrong predicted this season would be the last Crow communal buffalo hunt. With their major food source vanishing, Armstrong perceived the "future of these people does not look very bright." To meet the need and challenges to sustain the Crow, the agent recommended the government "persuade" and "control" the Indians for their own good.[495] He recognized the Crow preferred their "wild life" to civilized life but believed there were enough "sensible" ones who

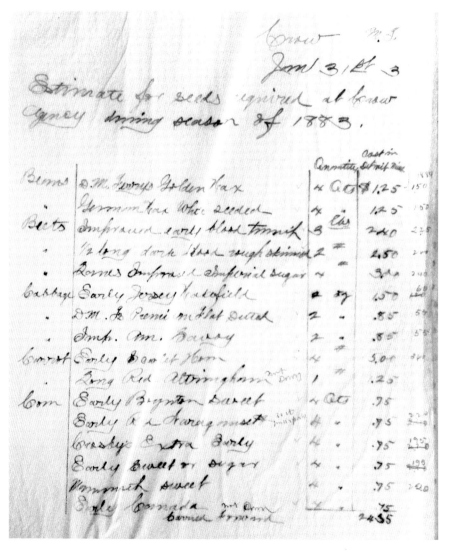

Seed purchase, January 31, 1883. *Bk1/Fd5 MC87 MHS.*

understood "the old times are past" and ready to settle down and farm.[496] This was "impossible" unless plans were firmed for their permanent home, he argued.[497]

The Buffalo

In 1851, it was estimated there were from seventy-five to over one hundred million buffalo. The Great Plains held four herds: the Northern, Republican, Arkansas and Texas. In 1871, an eastern tannery found buffalo hides as a great source for commercial leather. "Hide hunters" by the hundreds spread across the Plains, slaughtering buffalo at the rate of three million per year. By 1878, the southern herds were obliterated. By 1883, a scientific expedition could find only two hundred buffalo in the entire West. For the Plains Indians, this disappearance and loss of a great food source and resource was devastating.[498]

Buffalo meat was the main staple of the Native Americans' diet. Often the meat was split into sections, spread on racks to dry in the sun and turned often. At night, the meat was piled on the ground and covered with a buffalo robe. Excess blood was trodden out. In the morning, the meat was replaced on the racks with great care not to place it where meat was previously; otherwise it would spoil.

Pemmican was a winter diet stable. It consisted of lean meat cut into strips, roasted and then pounded. The meat was next soaked in water with ripened chokecherries. Added to this were boiled crushed bones. The resulting marrow was skimmed off and mixed with pounded meat. It was then put into buffalo heart skins until it got solid.[499]

Wild game, particularly buffalo, provided Native Americans many essentials: food, clothing, shelter and tools crafted from bone. One scholar counted eighty-seven different tools and implements that were made of bison parts, perhaps upward to even more than a hundred.[500]

According to one witness in 1877, smoked hide tipis filtered the sun, lending a "dim religious light," which also discouraged flies. Beds of buffalo robes were placed along the walls and the floor was swept clean as the palm of a hand. Sixteen hides were used for the average-sized lodge, although it is recorded the famous Crow leader Iron Bull had a lodge constructed of twenty-five hides.[501] Eight to sixteen people lived in one lodge.[502]

Armstrong was also combating secondary effects from declining wild game numbers. Tribal hunting under the 1868 treaty was permitted off the reservation on lands that were unoccupied. Keenly aware of diminishing wildlife inside the Crow Reservation, Armstrong kept a close tab on Crow hunting bands leaving the agency to ensure they didn't wander across reservation borders and into trouble.

Crazy Head was one who did encounter conflict. While wintering away from the agency in the Powder River country, two hundred horses were stolen from his band of thirty-five lodges. During the process of recapturing the herd, a Crow man, Round Iron, was killed.[503] According to one military officer, Crazy Head was "a bad man." If his people were hungry, "he will allow them to kill cattle and [this] may cause alarm along the whole frontier."[504]

Cattlemen accusing the Crow of stealing cattle and setting their range lands on fire demanded a reduction to the Crow reservation.[505] Armstrong found he gained not only the contempt of the stockmen but also the "bitter hatred of many folks in the vicinity."[506] He reported several trespassers to the U.S. attorney for cutting wood illegally on the reservation, often confiscating their product and selling it and placing the funds in an agency account.[507] When a fire of unknown cause on February 15, 1883, consumed the

Drying meat. *035B03F05.04 Bud Lake Coll. MHS.*

Iron Bull's camp on the Yellowstone. *ST 002.092, MHS.*

agency blacksmith and carpenter shop, it raised eyebrows, but no proof was discovered that unhappy sorts were out for justice.[508]

RELOCATION

As the weather eased, Armstrong continued to press for relocation, forwarding to his superior on May 8, 1883, plans for the new agency, "diminished" in size but "similar to the present one." The proposal included 50 log cabins for the Crow, a storeroom 110 by 26 feet and a granary and seed house 60 by 22 feet. The "Home Building doubled in size all totaling, $39, 566.94."[509]

An amended plan for the inclusion of a "play-ground" around the Home Building raised the total estimate to $40,402.19.[510] As for the physical location itself, Armstrong selected the site "eight miles below the mouth of Grass Lodge Creek on the west bank of the Little Horn river."[511]

A Senate committee sent west to learn of tribal conditions convened at the Absaroka Agency on August 7, 1883. Testimony from agency officials and Crow leaders covered a range of topics, among them discussions about relocating some of the Crow to the Big Horn. Plenty Coups declared, "The Crows are not fools yet.…They like to live in this country.…When we get cattle and farms we will have something to eat.[512]

When questioned about relocating their agency, Iron Bull, Two Belly and Thin Belly were suspicious more Crow property would be lost. Plenty Coups shared the same view. "I think the Great Father is trying to steal the agency and carry it into the lower country," he remarked.[513]

Agency personnel, miliary officials and others acquainted with the situation spoke affirmatively on the relocation. Most adamant was George Milburn, special Indian agent. He proclaimed, "No longer is there an unsettled frontier…[and] support by hunting no longer exists." He concluded it mandatory they settle on the most "eligible portion of their reserve.…The present site of the agency is in country illy adapted to…the plan of making farmers and grazer of these Indians, which they must become or starve."[514]

Several factors motivated the government decision to relocate both the agency and the Crow, one being Armstrong's prediction of the "inevitable" sale of their present agency and surrounding reservation.[515] Not only were adjacent lands getting "settled up" by whites in rapid manner,[516] but also looming was an expectation for "precious metals" discoveries on the reservation, all leading to potential trouble and pressure to remove the Crow.[517]

The agency buildings themselves, described Armstrong, were in a "dilapidated condition" without roofs, had adobe "washing away" and required further government expenditures.[518] Another factor was the Crow families who had already relocated and settled on their farms, suggesting in the near future a "discontinuance" or need to purchase subsistence rations. This lent well to the government's ultimate ideal, the Crow to become self-sustaining.[519]

Armstrong's pleas to relocate were heeded by a number of Crow such as Old Crow, who realized his hunting for subsistence days were over.[520] War Man, Iron Bull, Two Owl, Mrs. Tom Leforge and Porcupine[521] selected farm ground in the valley of the Big Horn,[522] followed by Plenty Coups, who perhaps

War Man. *035B01F04.02 Bud Lake Coll. MHS.*

Top: The Firelight Dance of Crow Indians by H.F. Farny. *From* Harper's Weekly, *December 15, 1883*.

Bottom: Perhaps a Crow ceremony before the dedication. *H-996, Haynes Coll. MHS.*

realized farming and stock raising were the only alternative to diminished game. He requested a "ranch of his own…on Pryor's Creek…There is no other place he wanted to live and have his home," wrote Armstrong."[523]

GOLDEN SPIKE

In the midst of all this was the celebration for the final spike in the Northern Pacific Railroad, binding Lake Superior in Michigan to Puget Sound in Washington, and the Crow were invited to participate. On September 8, 1883, the "Golden Spike" ceremony took place on Independence Creek between Garrison and Gold Creek, Montana, with notables General Ulysses S. Grant; Captain John Mullan; Secretary of State William M. Evarts; Secretary of the Interior Henry M. Teller; Northern Pacific president Henry Villard; former Northern Pacific president Frederick Billings; Governor Crosby of Montana; and governors from Dakota, Wisconsin, Oregon and Washington. Several international dignitaries from Germany and England were also in attendance.

Golden Spike Ceremony. Iron Bull (*standing center*), Mrs. Iron Bull (*with blanket at waist*) and Medicine Crow (*sitting center front*) others unidentified. *H-997, Haynes Coll. MHS.*

Twenty-two Crow representatives, including Chief Iron Bull, his wife, and three or four other women, were escorted to the ceremony by Tom Leforge. They traveled from the Absaroka Agency to Greycliff, Montana Territory. The Crow call this area Baa'hpalokape, Where the Cliffs Make a Bowl. It was a favorite campsite.[524] There, according to Leforge, "the railroad provided Pullman cars for us. No tepees were taken along. We had berths, plenty of room and plenty of food given to us. We were treated in grand style generally."[525] Two passenger trains arriving from Billings stopped at Greycliff for an exhibition dance by the Crow. Guests, particularly the Europeans, enjoyed this. When two more train sections arrived, another round of dancing resumed.[526]

Proceeding along to Gold Creek, an estimated crowd of 3,000 to 5,000 lined the tracks to watch the laying down of the last 1,200 feet of track until the last spike remained. According to one news account, the finest moment occurred when Iron Bull presented Henry Villard the spike, saying, "To you, President Villard—to you and your associates of the Northern Pacific road, Iron Bull, chief of the Crows, presents this spike, with the hope that you will drive it well home and thus have it bind the hearts of your red brethren to you and your enterprise as closely and as firmly as it binds your ties of steel the one to the other." When interpreted, applause and cries were shouted, "Good for the Indians," and "Three cheers for the Crows."[527]

HORSE RAIDS

At the same time Armstrong was anticipating construction on the new agency, and trying to sustain the Crow, five Piegan Indians stole thirty-five horses belonging to Plenty Coups on February 15, 1884. Fleeing north, the raiders continued to steal from white settlers, prompting a joint effort with the Crow to overtake the thieves, leading to the death of two white men. In a second horse raid near the Absaroka Agency, the Piegans made off with seventy horses.[528] During a third raid in March, the crafty thieves stole over one hundred Crow horses. In the process of recovery, a white man was killed. "They have robbed my Indians of not less than 500 horses," valued from $10 to $12,000, reported Armstrong.[529]

Pretty Horse, Louise Bompard and Top of the Moccasin, Crow farmers. *955-787 MHS.*

MOVING TO "NEW CROW"

Finally, "after two years to get the matter decided,"[530] Montana papers announced that the first week of April 1884, the Crow with "poor and weak" horses[531] and "twenty wagons"[532] were moving eastward out of the Stillwater Valley on a journey of about 170 miles[533] to their new agency location. First to go were 138 families, 985 people,[534] one-third of the tribe,[535] who previously had farmed or worked at various agency tasks. The remainder would stay to tend the agency fields and follow as headquarters and supplies became established.[536] Many were saddened by the move, especially some of the "women [who] openly cried and grieved for months when they were told they had to leave."[537]

They arrived at their destination on April 14. A temporary warehouse, sixteen by thirty-two feet, was constructed and families "assigned" to fifty-two previously constructed log cabins. Others were promised their own residences "as soon as possible." Armstrong was convinced their new "beginning is a good one." By August, he was "rejoicing" as nearly one hundred homesteads were inhabited by the Crow, coupled with a "nearly completed" agency and the remainder of the tribe on their way.[538] His optimism was premature, for expectations for the Crow to farm in earnest fell short, as not enough "sod" was turned over for planting, nor was there "enough seed of any kind." For those who did plant, they were late in doing so, and lack of timely rain followed by drying winds did not equate to a "large" bounty.[539] The reality was the Crow were hungry.

Chief Iron Bull elaborated on a former occasion he did what the "Great Father" asked of him. He undertook farming and pleaded, "My people got poor; I take care of my crop, and know how to use the hoe; my house is not good, but I live in it; our land is going away from us very fast....The buffalo and elk and deer are gone....Our children our starving. We want... cows that will have young ones, and we will put them at the foot of the mountains and all along the creek, and by the springs."[540]

This did not go unnoticed by Armstrong, who urged the commissioner of Indian affairs of the need to purchase a "great deal more subsistence supplies" for the Crow. He reminded the commissioner the friendly dispositioned Crow were "valuable" to the whites when most tribes were at war. He warned, however, "they will not sit down quietly and be starved." He reasoned until they become capable farmers, they require our assistance "<u>now</u>." He offered several suggestions to ease their transition, such as the construction of irrigation ditches and for yearly payments taken from the past land sale for the purchase of farming equipment.[541] By July, it was reported the Crows were "taking kindly" and working "with becoming pride."[542]

9

EDUCATION

Educational Challenges

With the inclusion of Article 7 in the 1868 treaty education of the Crow became a "necessity." It fell on the Indian agent to implement procedures for children between the age of six and sixteen to attend school. Complications and challenges to enforce attendance became readily apparent. Agents resorted to many means, from using white students to set an example to preparing a reading and spelling book with text in both Crow and English to "aid" the students.[543] Daily issues of stick candy to pupils were used as bribes,[544] as were one agent's attempt to boost school turnout by offering various chiefs and headmen employment.[545]

Another failed plan was bolstering enrollment of Crow children by band or group affiliation.[546] Tactics such as cutting and shortening Crow students' hair was found to thwart efforts, as the child was viewed a "ghost person," or someone in mourning, since such practices were customary for those grieving.[547] An attempt of dressing a few Crow students in white clothing failed by discouraging attendance from those attired in Native clothing.[548]

For incidents concerning students who fled from school, a horse, sugar and blankets were given for the return of one child.[549] As was the case with John, a Crow student taken out of school by relatives to go hunting, a message was sent by the agent to leading chiefs appealing for his return. Old Crow gave John's grandmother a horse as reward for his return.[550] Another family was threatened with loss of their food rations if their student didn't return to school.[551]

However, not all school reports were negative; several agents spoke highly of Crow students. "Their penmanship cannot be excelled anywhere under the same circumstances,"[552] boasted one, submitting writing examples to his superior as proof.

Another agent found both their penmanship and drawing skills "excelled" over white children.[553] Additionally, another agent noted the Crow students were "tractable, learn easy, but cannot be held in the school room as long as white children."[554] "I have never in my life…[witnessed] children who were more kinder to each other," expressed a third.[555]

Maintaining school enrollment numbers was a continual struggle for agents also facing cultural factors, most significantly, the Crow customary buffalo hunt. Their annual departure from the agency and vicinity interrupted school attendance.[556] The scenario was abundantly clear by 1872, as noted by a visiting government official describing the "day-school a failure." During winter, forty to sixty children are present he added, but "none are left" when the families depart for the hunt.[557] This thread resonated from frustrated agents. The Crow people remain on their reservation, or near the agency, "but a few months in the year," explained Agent Frost. "And many of them but a few weeks. They love the excitement of the chase. The first request of the young is "to go to buffalo." He added, "and so it is the last request of the aged."[558] This was corroborated by Agent Keller's observation when the grass turned green the Crow moved out "like a grand army" to the prairies for their annual buffalo hunt. A repeat effort was made in the fall.[559]

Other school interruptions were attributed to "constant warfare" between the Sioux and the Crow, leaving the Crow in an unsettled condition.[560] This later hindrance was confirmed by Blackfoot stating, "I want my own boy to learn to read" and for the people to become educated, but they could not do so while the Sioux were continually at war with them. "Our children will not look in books, that only hurts their eyes while they love so to read the war paint on their Brothers Robes."[561]

Illness such as scarlet fever and diphtheria also took their toll on enrollment numbers due to suspended schools as the Crow dispersed.[562]

Associated with the school was the "home," a structure of "limited" means but guided by a "patient" matron attending to fifteen to twenty Crow children. Here, the girls learned pursuits of baking bread, cooking and sewing. Boys were instructed in farm work, cutting wood and care of livestock.[563] One Crow student rose through the ranks as a carpenter's apprentice and another as assistant blacksmith.[564] Such training methods, instilling habits that "teach the brain to thin…and the hand to work," were considered an essential factor toward Indians' self-support.[565]

CARLISLE INDIAN SCHOOL

Endorsing this method to a new level was Colonel Richard Henry Pratt, a former officer in the Tenth Cavalry. After the Civil War, Pratt later became the jailer for seventy-two warriors from the Cheyenne, Kiowa, Comanche and Caddo Nations who were sent to the Fort Marion Prison in Florida. By the end of their term of incarceration (1878), Pratt had convinced seventeen prisoners to further their education by enrolling in the Hampton Institute in Virginia, a boarding school for "Negroes" designed to educate by teaching practical skills. At Hampton, Pratt began to lay the outline for a similar school, but exclusively for Indians. By mid-1879, Pratt had secured the use of a former cavalry post, Carlisle Barracks in central Pennsylvania. Here, he became founder and superintendent of Carlisle Indian School. His plan involved the removal of Indian children from the reservation, away from family and tribal influences, to integrate and assimilate them into white society through education and industrial skills.[566]

Agent A.R. Keller also believed educational opportunities and results at Carlisle were "much better" than offered at the agency and the means to "channel" Crow survival. He witnessed tribal members shunning their "medicine men" and turning to the agency physician as confirmation they were on the path of breaking "old prejudices and superstitions" and open for new ways.[567] Formal schooling would offer new possibilities, and though Keller during his tenure did make efforts to send a few boys east for instruction purposes, it became the responsibility of Agent Henry Armstrong to find a way.

Armstrong outlined his education "plan" in 1882 to his superior in Washington. He advocated removing and thus separating "entirely from the tribe" one hundred boys, aged twelve to eighteen, "who cannot speak a word of our language, and who are so wild that is not possible for us to teach them in the school or to reach them in any way."[568]

The agent was certain he could find "good families" in Ohio to take them in as their own sons and "teach them books, and the various arts, trades, and farming." After an absence of two or three years, he optimistically believed their return to the agency would foster a "sufficient number…competent to

Crow students: Fisher with Thomas, *NAA INV.06848300*; Anderson, *NAA INV.06877100*; Big Hair, *NAA INV.06840700*; Wallace, *NAA INV.06833200*.

manage the business affairs of this tribe."[569] However, the great plan failed, for Armstrong was "unable to persuade" any to go east."[570]

The following year, Armstrong was informed by the commissioner of Indian affairs of the twenty Crow students designated for Carlisle, half should be girls. The agent responded he was looking forward and "anxious" to visit the institution for "some ideas" to benefit his own agency work, then became crestfallen when learning he would not be escorting the

Top: John Wesley ledger art sketched prior to Carlisle departure. *Ledger Drawing 1930.45 Barstow Collection, MSUB Special Collections.*

Bottom: Inside print shop. *NAA INV.06801900.PhotoLot.81-82.*

Crow students: Hill, *Cumberland County Historical Society (CCHS) PA-CH1-001b*; Onion, *CCHS PA-CH2-092c*; Russell, *CCHS PA-CH1-085d*; Pretty Scalp, *CCHS PA-CH1-068a*; Stewart, *CCHS PA-CH1-038d*.

Crow "youths" on their journey to Carlisle.[571] Nor was he successful in fulfilling the request for ten girls, there being "only three" at the agency he favored. "Two of the three refused" to go, and in the end Armstrong was "compelled to give up." However, five young men and three boys did accept the proposition.[572] They departed the Absaroka Agency on February 22, 1883, and arrived at Carlisle on February 28.[573]

Carl Lieder became involved with the Carlisle Indian Printers. The printing program and resulting newspapers were popular among the local townsfolk, available at the Carlisle Post Office (at small cost) and by subscription throughout the country. The publications also provided Pratt with a platform from which to publicize his experiment and perpetuate his views on education.

Carlisle also offered an "outing" system allowing students the opportunities to live with and work for white families. This program aided Pratt's philosophy on how to acculturate Native Americans into mainstream society. Placements in the program occurred over the summer, though sometimes during the school year. Rather than risk sending students home, they were sent into various local communities, sponsored by families and put to work. Students were paid, with earnings deposited into their account at Carlisle. The platform grew quite popular for communities needing labor for minimal wages.

Crow, circa 1885. *Standing, left to right*: George Thomas, possibly Carl Leider and Charlie Fisher; *sitting*: Helen Onion, Persis Big Hair, unidentified and Lois Pretty Scalp. *CCHS BS-CH-038.*

145

Carlisle archives disclose another group of Crow youths departing the Absaroka Agency on November 13, 1883. The following entered Carlisle Indian School.[574]

I apologize for this sensitive subject. Boarding schools were often a traumatic experience for Native American students. Stripped of language, culture and heritage, the layers were peeled away to ultimately Americanize them. Disease and harsh conditions also took their toll, with hundreds dying; some remains were returned to their families. At Carlisle, 186 children are buried on the site today.

10

A LOOK INTO
THE ABSAROKA AGENCY

O ur graphic glimpse into the Absaroka Agency is very limited. To date, the only period illustration is a painting done in 1883 by noted artist George de Forest Brush. It was drawn on the back of a cigar box lid and given to Hugh Campbell, an agency farmer employee.[575] Depicted is the adobe brick warehouse and supply room. Butcher Creek, named for the slaughterhouse facilities there, is shown in the foreground. A few images of the agency in a state of decline have surfaced, as has a map of the agency drawn by Agent George Frost in July 1878. This map became the basis for a series of Absaroka Agency renderings accomplished by Daniel J. Glenn of Glenn and Glenn Architects for the Museum of the Beartooths in Columbus, Montana. Complete with a three-dimensional model housed in the museum, and building visuals, they aid in Absaroka Agency interpretation.

Newspaper accounts written by various early travelers spell out further details and confirmed Agent Clapp's boast in May 31, 1875, of finding a "beautiful"[576] agency location. This was corroborated a month later by a reporter calling himself "U Know." He was delighted with "the East Fork of the Rose Bud," finding the mountain stream beautifully clear. "The surroundings are indeed pleasant," he attested, "rolling, grassy hills stretch far into the distance."[577] The location is "admirable" wrote another traveler this same year. "Ten thousand acres, all of which lies adjacent to the Agency, can be irrigated."[578] A military officer in 1876 observed the agency occupied "an elevated plateau overlooking the valley."[579] The bounty near the agency locale is evident in Glenn's rendering of the complex and distant Beartooth Mountain vista.

Above: In 1882, George de Forest Brush (1854/1855–1941) lived among the Arapahoe and Shoshone in Wyoming and Crow in Montana. *MOB*.

Opposite, top: Agent George Frost map, drawn July 1878. *MOB*.

Opposite, bottom: Glenn rendering of agency, including "Doby Town" row of dwellings for white men married to Crow women. *MOB*.

A second "traveling correspondent" for Bozeman's *Avant Courier*, Fred M. Wilson, provides added details of his visit to the Absaroka Agency in 1878. "The whole is kept tidy as Government barracks on inspection day, and the streets and alleys as neat as a parade ground."[580] He observed the principal building is a "large adobe structure, which occupies three sides of a square." One portion was home to the agent and his family, another was filled by agency "attaches" and one served as storage for Indian supplies. A trading store occupied the remaining room, along with a "large stable" and blacksmith shop, a "row of one-story, white-washed dwellings,"[581] were occupied by white men employed at the agency and married to Crow women.[582] These dwellings, known as "Doby town,"[583] were in front of "the main entrance."[584] Nearby was the home for the Crow interpreter. This structure was of noted "importance at the Agency," for it served as "an Indian hotel, being the

148

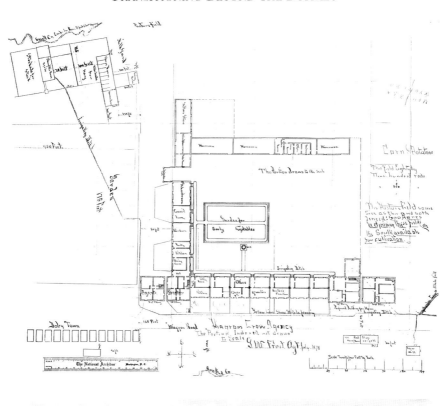

regular stopping place of small parties of Crows who are constantly visiting the Agency."[585] One photo has surfaced of a whitewashed agency dwelling; left to right are believed to be Charles T. Babcock, an agency trader, and Tom Kent, agency butcher and husband of What She Has Is Well Known. Seated may be Jack Mills, the cook. The standing man is unidentified.

Whitewashed adobe dwelling. *H52 Haynes Coll. MHS.*

The 1895 ruins. *Jim Annin Coll. MOB.*

To help one gain an idea of the rough-and-tumble sort often employed at the agency is in an account involving Babcock and two grizzly bear cubs he traded for. Evidently, one cub grew quite tame, while the other Babcock declared he would fight, thus allowing him to claim he "had a real hand to hand fight with a bear." Ignoring suggestions to arm himself with a knife proved unwise, for the bear clawed and lacerated the trader until he was profusely bleeding, thus ending the show.[586]

Remains of the agency in 1895 depict its extent. One row, 150 feet by 2 feet, consisted of many adobe chambers, including the council room, witness to life-altering discussions between Crow and government officials.[587] Employee Jirah Allen explained other chambers were "occupied by the doctor, clerk and other officers connected" to the agency. The cook's residence was on the "north wall and connected with the dining room." On the northeast was the traders store where Allen would work as "a trader's clerk for five years." The "walls had loop holes" for rifles he reminisced, and "not only built for protection, but the inside walls also served as the rear walls to the many rooms."[588] One end was topped by a two-story thirty-by-thirty-foot structure,[589] which the deteriorated view clearly shows.

F.M.W., a visitor to the Absaroka Agency in 1882, was impressed by his fifteen-mile journey to reach it. He found the Stillwater River "a clear, sparkling, mountain torrent, that surges impetuously over its rocky bed, and by its roar and ceaseless fretting seems emphatically to protest against the name it bears. On either side are rocky ledges, crowned by groves of pine trees which greatly add to the beauty of the landscape." At the agency, F.M.W. was greeted by "comforts and generous cheer" of the occupants and Agent Henry J. Armstrong. He keenly observed the agency buildings "are built in the form of a square, inside of which is a broad, smooth court."[590] Situated in the center of the "stockade" was a "large" building that served as the children's home; however, an August 1883 fire destroyed it.[591]

Most visitors, including Charles Hallock, agreed the Absaroka Agency was indeed picturesque. During his travels in 1882, he described the agency buildings arranged "in Mexican style on three sides of a plaza or court, with an arched entrance in the center; a part of the court is devoted to a kitchen garden which is irrigated by acequias or ditches." A warehouse formed the fourth side of the plaza, with numerous buildings and a sawmill, outside the "plaza." Ambling to a nearby small stream, Hallock noted an "Indian burying ground, with the boxed remains of the dead perched on scaffolds, and some in the forked trees." He observed burial caskets fashioned "from merchandise boxes obtained from the post trader." One crate was "marked DW" for "Improved Double Weight." Hallock explained not all Crow remains were buried in caskets or scaffolds. "In a central part of the ground is a full-sized skin tepee, the lodging of a chief while he lived, and now inclosing the mortuary remains of the honored dead. There are also a few graves of white people marked by marble slabs, showing that the Crow and their pale-faced friends fraternize in death, even as they do in life."[592] Hallock went on to describe the Crow's "permanent" village located about a mile above the agency; it comprised about two hundred lodges, but that number often varied. "Some of the lodges have large fenced gardens attached, the best of which belongs to a fine old chief named Iron Bull." However, the pressures and effects from hide hunters on wild game, especially buffalo, were evidenced in Hallock's observation that with the "present scarcity of elk and buffalo skins, canvas is being largely substituted for lodge coverings." He found a certain gaiety to camp life among the Crow. Children "race ponies through the camp, three or four little urchins on a single beast. The old men smoke in quiet groups, while the women occupy themselves with domestic duties." However, the visitor took offense to the "gangs" of dogs "gaunt and staveling [*sic*] of every hue and size…making night hideous with howls."[593]

A glimpse of a period Crow village near the Absaroka Agency by F.J. Haynes. Seated, in a white hat; Colonel Jirah Allen, scout, trader, interpreter and agency clerk. Standing back row with white hat is Barney Bravo (Prevo, Big Nose), intrepreter; to his right is Two Belly. To Bravo's left is Medicine

Top: Crow burials. *H-555 Haynes Coll MHS.*

Bottom: A Crow village near the Absaroka Agency. *H-550 Haynes Coll. MHS.*

Crow. Next to him is his wife, Sacred Mountain Sheep, with baby. Astride his horse is Poor Elk (Thin Elk).

POST ABSAROKA AGENCY PERIOD

On September 16, 1951, a celebration was held for the centennial anniversary of the signing of the treaty of 1851. Upward of eight thousand people lined the streets of Absarokee, Montana, for a parade, headed by Plainfeather and George Goes Ahead followed by tribal members dancing on a float. A program followed at Clarence Smith's Circle C ranch near the former Absaroka Agency. Public addresses were made by John Provinse of Washington, D.C., assistant commissioner of Indian affairs, and Robert Yellowtail, president of the Crow Tribal Council. A buffalo barbecue feast rounded out the day.

A granite monument on Highway 78 across from the former site of the Absaroka Agency was placed and dedicated in 1964 in memory of Senator Joseph Burt Annin and Janet Annin by sons Jim, Burt and Doug Annin. Dr. Joseph Medicine Crow gave an address to the gathering. In the fall of

Annin dedication. *MOB.*

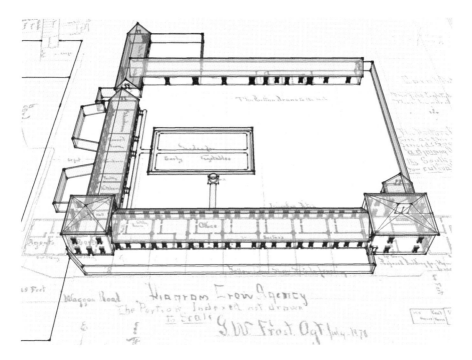

Glenn's graphic design taken from an overlay of Agent Frost's map. It depicts the court and building in the form of a square. *MOB.*

2010, Medicine Crow returned to this site along with his son, Ron, and his wife, Gloria.

In the mid-1980s, an archaeological survey was conducted for the Montana Department of Transportation along Montana Highway 78 to determine if any vestiges of the former agency would be destroyed by proposed highway construction. The assessment, based on the lack of surface finds, concluded that preexisting highway construction had already disturbed the remains. Around 2000, the MDT took steps once again to widen this section of highway. An archaeological firm, Aaberg Cultural Resources Consulting Services, was brought in as pursuant to the 1990 Native American Grave Protection and Repatriation Act. Steve Aaberg, president of the firm, and crew did small-scale testing along the corridor with probes, revealing enough artifacts remained to merit further tests. In the summer of 2006, in cooperation with the MDT, which by law has to consider the effects of projects on historical sites, Aaberg conducted a magnetometer survey, measuring magnetic signatures of objects beneath the surface. The results recorded on a computer-generated map showed underground anomalies in the form of a rectangle. Although Aaberg didn't know exactly what they were, he discovered the rectangle footprint matched the agency compound map drawn by Agent Frost in 1878. Ironically, the invaluable map was discovered in the Montana Historical Museum's archives by MDT historian Jon Axline. Further work revealed artifacts, including bones and beads, along both sides of the highway and warranted a full-fledged archaeological excavation.

In the summer of 2011, Steve Aaberg and crew began excavation of the site. Their first discovery was the northwest corner of the agency foundation; workers continued uncovering segments of rooms, including the agent's, doctor's and clerk's office, all matching the 1878 map. Also uncovered were thousands of butchered bone fragments, beads, bottles, cartridge casings and hide scrappers, which will be catalogued.[594] In 2011, an event sponsored by Extreme History, the Museum of the Beartooth and others gave Crow elders and others interested an opportunity to view the site. Since then, many more school and group tours have piqued public interest.

Both Fort Parker and the Absaroka Agency are a significant, if not tragic link, in Crow history. In 2016, The Extreme History Project, spearheaded by Marsha Fulton and Crystal Alegria, announced a fifteen-acre purchase of Fort Parker by the Archaeological Conservancy. The agreement will ensure perpetual protection of the site from any purchase or development. The plan also called for development of education and interpretation on the site. While the Museum of the Beartooths houses and provides a significant interpretation on the Absaroka Agency, the fate of the agency site at this time is undetermined. A portion of the author's proceeds from the sale of this book will be dedicated to preserving and interpreting the Absaroka Agency history.

The Crow Tribe's migration from the Absaroka/Beartooth foothills to the banks of the Big Horn River was the result of events and policy beyond their control. The Crow went from a rich, self-sustaining culture dependent on buffalo to a "new beginning," conditional on farming and, later, stock raising.[595] Agriculture provided the means for a "settled residence," the very essence Agent Armstrong and the U.S. government deemed key to the Crows' permanence, future growth and independence.[596]

Filling the years 1869 to 1884 were eight separate Crow agents, tenure for some less than a year, creating a lack of continuity or an articulated program. Each new appointment brought a different set of values,

At the Absaroka Agency site and viewing foundation ruins is Elias Goes Ahead (*center, with straw hat*). *Author photo*.

Top: Participants, including Janis Eckert, viewing artifacts uncovered from agency. *MOB*.

Bottom: Joe Medicine Crow at the Museum of the Beartooths comparing floral patterns on his cane to those from the Absaroka Agency period. *Author photo*.

personalities and experiences, creating a situation with no neutral ground or reliable cohesion for the Crow. Agents filed papers and reports, some to defend their actions, others to question policy. Excitedly, they wrote of Crow warriors turning to walk behind the plow. But the reality of the change is found in some of the mound of paperwork. Prior to relocating to present-day Crow Agency, of the 3,200 Crow members, just 70 families in 1883 were involved in agriculture. They owned 620 head of cattle, pale in comparison to their past ownership of 12,000 horses, their greatest pride, not to mention wealth.

With the move to the Big Horn, numbers increased to 236 families actively farming, with a six-fold increase in cattle.[597] Coinciding with near decimated buffalo herds and reduced government food rations, the Crow had but little choice to settle on allotments, acreage thought sufficient by the government. But unless every cow was milked, making a living was near impossible.[598]

Settlers soon found the attractive Rosebud, Rock Creek and Stillwater Valley and coveted it, thus leading to negotiations with the Crow for a land sale in 1890. At stake were 1.8 million acres in the western portion of their reservation, including the lands of the former Absaroka Agency. A sale price of $946,000 was reached, with a bulk of the funding, $552,000, to be appropriated toward a twenty-year annuity payment of $12 per Crow member.[599] Another $275,000 was marked for irrigation projects to support Indian farming near the new Crow Agency. Crow who already owned allotments on the newly ceded reservation had three years to either keep the parcel or surrender it for a new one on the retained portion. Provisions for comparable improvements on the new selections would be paid for. The agreement was ratified by Congress on March 3, 1891.[600]

Months later, a modification to the agreement was drawn up on August 27, 1892, and ratified on October 15, 1892. It clarified the number, location and ownership of Crow allotments made prior to the land cessation. At this juncture, a number of Crow relinquished their allotments in their old homeland for a future near their brethren on the reduced reservation.[601]

There were grim times for the Crow in the new corner of their reservation based near present-day Crow Agency. Decades of agricultural challenges were faced by the tribe, including costly irrigation projects, cattle and sheep leases, and large-scale farming by non-Crow members, land allotments, private land sales, grazing districts and water right issues.[602]

Hunts to Die's family had allotments on the ceded portion of the reservation, later relinquished. Pictured here is son Swallow Bird. X-*34138*, *Denver Public Library*.

However, just as Crow ancestral village farmers once regenerated themselves to become Plains hunters, the new Reservation Crow understood their future was linked also to their ability to adapt while maintaining their legacy and culture. They labored, prevailed, adapted and remain Indians of the Crow Nation today.

NOTES

1. Children of the Large Beaked Bird

1. Medicine Crow, *From the Heart*, 13, 18–20; Lopez, "Shiipdeetdeesh," 11; McCleary, "History of the Apsaalooke," 119.
2. McCleary, *Crow Indian Rock Art*, 22–23.
3. Bill Yellowtail to author, March 5, 2020.
4. Medicine Crow, *From the Heart*, 2.
5. McCleary, *Crow Indian Rock Art*, 20.
6. The author has recognized both the River and Mountain Crow dialects.
7. McCleary, "History of the Apsaalooke," 119.
8. McCleary, *Crow Indian Rock Art*, 24.
9. Smith, "Politics and the Crow Indian Land," 24–25; Hoxie, *Parading Through History*, 62–66.
10. Hoxie, *Parading Through History*, 86–88; Brown, *Plainsmen of the Yellowstone*, 127–28.
11. Brown, *Plainsmen of the Yellowstone*, 129.
12. Prucha, *American Indian Policy in Crisis*, 15; Utley, *Indian Frontier*, 106.
13. Oman, "Beginning of the End," 37.
14. Ibid.
15. Not to be confused with Fort Kearny, Nebraska.
16. Dr. Timothy McCleary, PhD, department head, General Studies Department, Little Big Horn College, to author.
17. Humpherys, "Crow Indian Treaties," 77.

18. Ibid.
19. Algier, *Crow and the Eagle*, 219.
20. Humpherys, "Crow Indian Treaties," 76–78.
21. Ibid., 79.
22. "Treaty with the Crows, 1868" (Treaty of Fort Laramie, 1868) 15 Stat. 635, May 7, 1868, ratified July 25, 1868, proclaimed August 12, 1868, in Kappler, *Indian Affairs*, 2:1008–11.
23. The main body of River Crow did not attend. However, they signed their own treaty on July 15, 1868, for a reservation in the Milk River region of northern Montana. The treaty was never ratified (Algier, *Crow and the Eagle*, 224–25).
24. During the next three weeks, other tribes signed similar treaties. The forts were closed and Red Cloud signed a treaty for the Sioux in November.

2. Fort Parker

25. Kappler, *Indian Affairs*, 2:1008–12.
26. Article 3, Kappler, *Indian Affairs*.
27. Alfred Sully, Superintendent of Indians, September 21, 1869, to Ely S. Parker, r489-NA234, Microfilm M234, U.S. Office of Indian Affairs, Letter Received, 1824–1880, National Archives and Records Administration [hereafter NA234].
28. Ibid.
29. Agent E. M. Camp to Sully, August (no date), 1870, Annual report of the Commissioner of Indian Affairs [hereafter ARCIA].
30. Marquis, *First Crow Agency*.
31. Camp to Sully, August 1870, ARCIA.
32. Agent Fellows D. Pease to Francis A. Walker, CIA, January 9, 1872, Fellows D. Pease Diary, Carbon County Historical Society, Red Lodge, MT (CCHS).
33. Camp to Sully, August 1870, ARCIA.
34. Ibid.
35. Pease to J.A. Viall, Superintendant of Indians Montana, August 31, 1871, ARCIA.
36. *Avant Courier*, February 29, 1872.
37. Wyndham-Quin, *Great Divide*, 61.
38. Rust, *Lost Fort Ellis*, 38.
39. Prucha, *American Indian Policy in Crisis*, 50.

40. *Montana Free Press* 8. no. 12 (Red Lodge, MT, 1998), 26–39, CCHS.

41. Pease to Viall, November 14–15, 1870, Pease Diary, CCHS.

42. Pease to Viall, August 31, 1871, ARCIA.

43. Pease, August 31, 1871.

44. *Fourth Annual Report of the Board of Indians Commissioners* [hereafter *Fourth Report*], 73.

45. Pease to Viall, August 31, 1871, ARCIA.

46. Pease, August 31, 1871.

47. Brown, *Plainsmen of the Yellowstone*, 195–96.

48. Pease to Walker, May 25, 1872, Pease Diary, CCHS.

49. Utley, *Lance and the Shield*, 117.

50. Hyde, *Red Cloud's Folk*, 24.

51. Medicine Crow, *From the Heart*, 64.

52. Pease to Viall, August 31, 1871, ARCIA.

53. U.S. Congress, *Congressional Globe*, 42nd Congress, 2nd Session, 1871–72, 1596. The bill passed both the House and Senate, March 3, 1873.. S. Congress, *Congressional Globe*, 42nd Congress, 3rd Session, 1343, 2205, 2209.

54. Pease to Viall, September 1, 1872, ARCIA, 278.

55. *Fourth Report*, 57.

56. Ibid., 73–74.

57. Ibid., 10.

58. *Avant Courier*, November 7, 1872.

59. *Globe*, 3rd Session, 1309.

60. *Fourth Report*, 72.

61. Humpherys, "Crow Indian Treaties," 87.

62. A third band was a derivative of the Mountain Crow called Kicked in the Bellies; McCleary, *Crow Indian Rock Art*, 22–23.

63. Pease, August 31, 1871, ARCIA; Viall to H.R. Clum, Acting Com., September 15, 1871, ARCIA, 415.

64. Pease to Viall, December 13, 1870, Pease Diary CCHS; Viall to Clum, September 15, 1871, ARCIA, 278.

65. Hoxie, *Parading Through History*, 100–101.

66. *Fourth Report*, 69, 72.

67. Delano to Smith, May 14, 1873, ARCIA, 1873, 113.

68. Prucha, *American Indian Policy in Crisis*, 68–69.

69. Pease to Smith, September 28, 1873, ARCIA, 1873.

70. Cree, *Fifth Annual Report of the Board* [hereafter *Cree Report*].

71. Ibid.

72. Wyndham-Quin, *Great Divide*, 67.

73. *Cree Report.*

74. "The Crow Indians Talked Out of Their Reservation, The Crow Indians Plucked," *New York Herald*, September 27, 1873.

75. Delano to Smith, October 31, 1873, r495-NA234.

76. Doane Report, November 19, 1874 r498-NA234.

77. Delano to Smith, September 20, 1873, r495-NA234.

78. Cross report, November 26, 1873, r497-NA234; Wright to Smith, November 29, 1873, r497-NA234, 49.

79. Doane Report, r498-NA234, 28.

80. Doane Report, 27; Belknap to Secretary of Interior [hereafter SecInt], December 31, 1873, r500-NA234.

81. Scott, *Splendid on a Large Scale*, 277–80.

82. Blackfoot to President Grant, December 5, 1873, r500-NA234.

83. Pease to Parker, August 31, 1871, ARCIA; Pease to Viall, September 1, 1872, ARCIA.

84. Prucha, *Great Father*, 63.

85. *Fourth Report*, 5.

86. Delano to Smith, September 20, 1873, r495-NA234.

87. *Cree Report*, 112.

88. *Helena Weekly Herald*, October 9, 1873.

89. Pease to Smith, November 26, 1873 r495-NA234

90. *Chicago Daily Tribune*, October 15, 1873.

91. Medicine vouchers, October 11, 1873, r500-NA234.

92. Telegram from Pease, October 13, 1873, r495-NA234.

93. "The Indian Council 10-Day, An Official Talk with the Crows. What They Ask of Their Great Father," *Evening Star*, October 21, 1873.

94. Crow Delegation Report, October 21, 1873, r495-NA234.

95. "Indian Council 10-Day."

96. *Alexandria Gazette*, October 25, 1873.

97. Ibid.

98. Crow Delegation Council with CIA, October 29, 1873, r495-NA234.

99. "Fourteen Savages at the Grand Central Hotel," *New York Herald*, November 3, 1873.

100. Pease to Smith, November 1, 1873, r495-NA234; Invoice, November 8, 1873, r495-NA234.

101. Delegation Council, October 29, 1873, r495-NA234.

102. Pease to Smith, November 7, 1873, r495-NA234.

103. Pease, November 7, 1983; Crow Delegation Report, October 21, 1873; Delegation Council, October 29, 1873.

104. Pease to Smith, November 26, 1873, r495-NA 234.
105. Potts to President, December 2, 1873, r495-NA234.
106. Blackfoot to President Grant, December 5, 1873, r500-NA234.
107. Koury, *Guarding the Carroll Trail*, 9.
108. Gray, *Custer's Last Campaign*, 108; Silliman, "Carroll Trail," 2–17.
109. Hoxie, *Parading Through History*, 104; Algier, *Crow and the Eagle*, 285–86; Brown, *Plainsmen*, 215, 431.
110. James Wright to Delano, r496-NA234.
111. Wright to B.R. Cowen, Asst. SecInt, January 4, 1873, r 496-NA234.
112. Wright to Smith, March 11, 1873, r496-NA234.
113. Wright, to Smith, March 10, 1873, r496-NA 234.
114. Found in "Brief of Contents," Pease, April 30, 1873, Register of Letters Received and Sent, Records of the Crow Indian Agency, MT, National Archives-Denver [hereafter RG 75].
115. Pease, April 30, 1873.
116. Marquis, *Memoirs of a White Crow*, 34–35.
117. Ibid., 40–41.
118. "Mary Kent," *Livingston Enterprise*, August 20, 1910.
119. Doyle, "Home Land."
120. Wright to Smith, March 10, 1873, CIA, r495-NA234; r496-NA234.
121. Marquis, *Memoirs of a White Crow*, 58.
122. Ibid., 44.
123. Wright to Smith, May 13, 1874, r500-NA234.
124. Wright to Smith, October 12, 1874, r500-NA234.
125. *Cree Report*.
126. Wright to Smith, October 30, 1874, r500-NA234.
127. Wright to Smith, March 11, 1873, r496-NA234.
128. Wright to Smith, March 29, 1873, r496-NA234.
129. *Sixth Annual Report Board of Indian Commissioners*, September 15, 1874, 54.
130. Cross to Wright, April 5, 1874; Wright to Smith, May 13, 1874, r500-NA234.
131. Kennedy, "Whoop-Up Trail," 1991.
132. Topping, *Chronicles*, 99.
133. Brekke, "Historical Overview of Benson's," 8.
134. Brown, *Plainsmen of the Yellowstone*, 432.
135. Wright to Smith, September 21, 1874, ARCIA.
136. Wright to Smith, May 20, 1874; October 12, 1874, r500-NA234.
137. Wright to Smith, May 20, 1874; October 12, 1874, r500-NA234.
138. SecInt circular, May 11, 1874, r500-NA234.

139. Wright to Smith, May 20, 1874, r500-NA234.

140. Marquis, *Memoirs of a White Crow*, 41–43.

141. "From Bensons' Landing," *Avant Courier*, April 30, 1875.

142. Crow historian Alden Big Man to author, October 10, 2023.

143. "Another Indian Raid," *Avant Courier*, July 31, 1874.

144. Burlingame, "Andrew Jackson Hunter Family," 9.

145. Wright to Smith, March 10, 1873, r496-NA234.

146. Wright to Smith, ARCIA, September 21, 1874.

147. Wright to Smith, July 14, 1874, r500-NA234; Wright to Smith, ARCIA, September 21, 1874.

148. *Cree Report*.

149. Wright to Smith, ARCIA, September 21, 1874.

150. Clapp to Smith, December 22, 1874, RG 75.

3. Agent Dexter Clapp and the Absaroka Agency

151. *Avant Courier*, December 4, 1874.

152. Clapp to Smith, September 10, 1875, ARCIA.

153. Clapp to Smith, December 22, 1874, RG 75, RCIA.

154. Clapp to E.P. Smith, March 5, 1875; Clapp to J.Q. Smith, March 6, 1876, RG 75.

155. "The New Crow Agency," *Avant Courier*, May 21, 1875.

156. Special Order No. 67, June 26, 1875, Captain D.W. Benham, r503-NA234.

157. June 29, 1875, Captain George Tyler from Benham, r503-NA234.

158. Clapp to E.P. Smith, September 27, 1875, RG 75.

159. Colonel John Gibbon to Department of Dakota, June 21, 1875, r503-NA234.

160. J.V. Bogert to Benham, June 18, 1875, r503-NA234.

161. Benham to Assistant Adjutant General (AAG), June 18, 1875.

162. Clapp to J.Q. Smith, March 6, 1876, RG 75.

163. White, "The Crow Indians and Their Reservation," *Avant Courier*, January 22, 1875.

164. *Cree Report*, 117.

165. Major N.B. Sweitzer to AAG Dakota, April 15, 1874, r500-NA234.

166. Curtis, *North American Indian*, 4:198.

167. Wright to E.P. Smith, June 9, 1874, r500-NA234.

168. Colonel John Gibbon, June 21, 1875, r503-NA234; Captain George L. Tyler, June 29, 1875, to Acting AAG, Montana, r503-NA234.

169. Sweitzer to AAG, Dakota, January 10, 1874, r500-NA234

170. Alden Big Man Jr. to author, February 13, 2023.

171. Clapp to Smith, March 5, 1875, r501-NA234.

172. Clapp to Smith, April 12, 1875, RG 75.

173. Clapp to Smith, May 4, 1875, r502-NA234; "The New Crow Agency," *Avant Courier*, June 11, 1875.

174. Clapp to Smith, April 12, 1875, RG 75.

175. "The New Crow Agency," *Avant Courier*, June 11, 1875.

176. White Calfee, Burlingame Collection 2245, Box 15, folder 27, MSU, Special Collections, Bozeman, MT. Information in this paragraph is taken from a manuscript, "Notes from a talk taken with Mr. White Calfee," including the interviewer's notes.

177. Clapp to Smith, May 31, 1875, RG 75.

178. "New Crow Agency," May 21, 1875.

179. Allen, "Building of Crow Indian Agency."

180. *Bozeman Times*, May 7, 1875.

181. Clapp to Smith, June 13, 1875, RG 75.

182. Clapp to Smith, May 31, 1875, RG 75.

183. Clapp, May 31, 1875.

184. Clapp to Smith, September 27, 1875, RG 75.

185. Clapp to Potts, June 10, 1875, RG 75.

186. Marquis, *Memoirs of a White Crow*, 110.

187. Clapp, September 27, 1875.

188. Also recorded as 200 by 26 feet, September 10, 1875, Clapp to Smith, RG 75.

189. Clapp to Smith, July 1, 1875, RG 75.

190. Clapp to Smith, July 27, 1875, RG 75.

191. Allen, *Columbus News*, October 20, 1927.

192. "The New Agency," *Avant Courier*, July 30, 1875.

193. Allen, October 20, 1927.

194. Clapp to Smith, July 1, 1875, RG 75.

195. Clapp to Potts and Sweitzer, June 10, 1875, RG 75.

196. Clapp to Smith, July 5, 1875, RG 75.

197. Also spelled Trojio.

198. Clapp to Smith, July 5, 1875, RG 75.

199. Marquis, *Memoirs of a White Crow*, 119.

200. Ibid., 116–18.

201. Agency Clerk, W.Y. Smith to Charles Rich, July 2, 1875, r503-NA234.

202. W.Y. Smith to Rich, July 2 and 3, 1875, r503-NA234.

203. Clapp to E.P. Smith, July 5, 1875, RG 75.

204. W.Y. Smith to Rich, July 2, 1875, r503-NA234.

205. Clapp to E.P. Smith, September 10, 1875, RG 75; *Helena Weekly Herald*, July 15, 1875.

206. W.Y. Smith to Rich, July 4, 1875, r503-NA234.

207. Smith, July 4, 1875; Brown, *Plainsmen of the Yellowstone*, 234.

208. Smith to Rich, 2:30 a.m., July 5, 1875, r503-NA234.

209. Smith, July 5, 1875.

210. Clapp to Smith, September 27, 1875, RG 75.

211. Mileage Tyler from Benham, June 29, 1875, r503-NA234; Clapp to Smith, September 10, 1875, RG 75.

212. Clapp to Sweitzer, May 17, 1875; Clapp to Smith, May 31, 1875; Clapp to Potts, July 9, 1875; Clapp to Smith, September 10, 1875, RG 75.

213. Clapp to Potts, July 9, 1875, RG 75.

214. Clapp, July 9, 1875.

215. Alden Big Man Jr. to author, February 13, 2023.

216. Potts to Smith, June 18, 1875; Clapp, September 10, 1875.

217. Potts to Delano, July 8, 1875, r503-NA234.

218. Potts, July 9, 1875, r503-NA234.

219. Alfred H. Terry to Delano, August 22, 1875, r503-NA234.

220. O.D. Green from Benham, July 8, 1875, r503-NA234.

221. Switzer, July 5, 1875, r503-NA234; August 22, 1875, Terry to Delano, August 22, 1875, r503-NA234.

222. Clapp to Smith, September 10, 1875, RG 75.

223. Clapp to Smith, August 4, 1875, RG 75.

224. Clapp to Smith, September 10, 1875, RG 75.

225. Clapp, September 10, 1875; Clapp to Smith, September 1, 1876, ARCIA.

226. Clapp to Smith, August 4, 1875, RG 75.

227. Clapp to Smith, August 31, 1875, RG 75.

228. Clapp, September 10, 1875.

229. Pease to Smith, October 5, 1875, RG 75.

230. Clapp to Smith, June 23, 1875, RG 75.

231. Clapp, June 23, 1875.

232. Clapp to John Q. Smith, March 25, 1876, RG 75.

233. Clapp, March 25, 1876.

234. Potts to Cowen, August 20, 1875, r502-NA234.

235. Potts to Delano, September 27, 1875, r502-NA234.

236. Potts, September 27, 1875.

237. "Gallatin County and the Crow Reservation," *Helena Weekly Herald*, October 7, 1875.

238. Ibid.
239. Ibid.
240. "The Crow Reservation," *Helena Weekly Herald*, April 13, 1876.
241. "AN OBNOXIOUS ENCROACHMENT," *New North-west*, November 26, 1875.
242. "The Crow Reservation," *Helena Weekly Herald*, November 18, 1875.
243. Citizen letter to President Grant, November 12, 1875, r505-NA234.
244. "The Crow Reservation Extension," *Helena Weekly Herald*, November 25, 1875.
245. Clapp to Smith, January 5, 1876, RG 75.
246. "Crow Reservation, The Order of Revocation," *Avant Courier*, March 31, 1876.
247. Clapp to J.Q. Smith, March 25, 1876, RG 75.
248. Clapp to Smith, January 5, 1876, RG 75.
249. Benham to Fort Shaw, June 29, 1875, r503-NA234.
250. Sweitzer to Department of Dakota. January 10, 1875, r500-NA234.
251. Sweitzer, January 20, 1875.
252. Ibid.
253. Tyler to Benham, June 29, 1875, r 503-NA234.
254. "Notes on our Trip to Fort Pease," *Avant Courier*, March 31, 1876.
255. McLemore, "Fort Pease," 19–21; Gray, *Custer's Last Campaign*, 118.
256. Educator and author Dr. Tim McCleary to author.
257. Ibid.
258. Gray, *Custer's Last Campaign*, 226; McLemore, "Fort Pease," 17.
259. Jirah Allen to Frank Shively, February 12, 1927, Harlan Conroy Family.
260. Brown, *Plainsmen of the Yellowstone*, 222.
261. McLemore, "Fort Pease," 22–23.
262. Clapp to Benham, Fort Ellis, January 10, 1876, r.505-NA 234.
263. Alden Big Man to author.
264. Gray, *Custer's Last Campaign*, 126.
265. McCormick and Dexter to Potts, February 18, 1876, r 505-NA234.
266. Brown, "Muddled Men," 37.
267. Brisbin to Clapp, February 20, 1876, r 504-NA 234.
268. Brisbin, February 20, 1876.
269. Alden Big Man to author.
270. Brisbin.
271. Gray, *Custer's Last Campaign*, 127–29.
272. Bradley, *March of the Montana Column*, 26–27.
273. Gray, *Custer's Last Campaign*, 130.

4. Scouts and Battles

274. Ibid., 123–30.

275. Ibid., 134; Gray, *Centennial Campaign*, 40.

276. *Cree Report*.

277. Nabokov, *Two Leggings*, 186.

278. *Cree Report*.

279. Alden Big Man to author, February 13, 2023.

280. Big Man, "Crow History," 101.

281. Ibid., 105.

282. Bradley, *March of the Montana Column*, 40.

283. Ibid., 41.

284. Ibid., 42.

285. Ibid., 44–45.

286. Ibid., 48–49.

287. Ibid., 87–89; Marquis, *Memoirs of a White Crow*, 210, 216.

288. Mangum, *Battle of the Rosebud*, 32–42.

289. Bourke, *On the Border*, 302.

290. Finerty, *War-Path and Bivouac*, 104.

291. Ibid., 103–5.

292. Mangum, *Battle of the Rosebud*, 43.

293. Bradley, *March of the Montana*, 143.

294. Viola, *Little Bighorn Remembered*, 111.

295. Ibid., 130, 154, 158–59.

296. Libby, *Arikara Narrative*, 80, 86–93.

297. Marquis, *Custer, Cavalry and Crows*, 71; Viola, *Little Bighorn Remembered*, 117.

298. Gray, *Custer's Last Campaign*, 351–52; Bradley, *March of the Montana*, 152–53.

299. Bradley, *March of the Montana*, 156–57; Marquis, *Custer, Cavalry and Crows*, 66.

300. Gray, *Custer's Last Campaign*, 373–80.

301. Bradley, *March of the Montana*, 155.

302. Marquis, *Custer, Cavalry and Crows*, 72.

303. Big Man, "Curly."

304. Mardell Hogan to author, July 27, 2020.

305. *Helena Weekly Herald*, June 22, 1876; *Avant Courier*, September 29, 1876.

306. Clapp to John Q. Smith, September 1, 1876, ARCIA.

307. Petitioners to Smith, December 6, 1876, r504-NA234.

308. Thomas Jones, January (no date) 1876, r504-NA234.

309. Carpenter to Smith, October 26, 1876, r504-NA234.

5. *Agents James Carpenter and George Frost*

310. John Q. Smith, CIA, October 30, 1876, ARCIA.

311. Ibid.

312. Ibid.

313. Carpenter to Smith, August 24, 1876, r504-NA234; "Nominations," *Cheyenne Daily Leader*, August 5, 1876.

314. Carpenter to Smith, September 1, 1876, r504-NA.

315. Carpenter to Smith, October 26, 1876, r504-NA.

316. Carpenter to Smith, November 26, 1876, r504-NA234.

317. Carpenter to Smith, February 17, 1877, r506-NA234.

318. Carpenter to Smith, January 20, 1877, r506-NA234.

319. Carpenter to Smith, January 26, 1877, r506-NA234.

320. Carpenter, January 20, 1877.

321. Ibid.

322. Ibid.

323. *Avant Courier*, March 1, 1877.

324. Carpenter to Smith, January 29, 1877, r506-NA234.

325. "The Crow Indians," *Avant Courier*, December 26, 1878.

326. Carpenter to Smith, June 6, 1877, RCIA-MC 87, Book 1, Montana Historical Society (MHS) [hereafter MC87].

327. *Avant Courier*, July 12, 1877; George Frost to Smith, July 13, 1877, r506-NA 234.

328. "Clarks Fork" and "Personal," *Helena Weekly Herald*, August 2, 1877.

329. Frost to Smith, August 17, 1877, ARCIA.

330. Frost to Smith, July 24, 1877, Bx1/Fd2, MC87.

331. Frost to Smith, August 9, 1877, Bx1/Fd2, MC87.

332. Frost to Smith, August 30, 1877, r506-NA234.

333. "The Crow Indians Loyal," *Avant Courier*, September 13, 1877.

334. Linderman, *Plenty-Coups*, 142–43.

335. Frost to Smith, September 12, 1877, r506-NA234.

336. Alden Big Man to author, June 2, 2023.

337. Frost to Smith, September 7? 1877 (date has faded), Bx1/Fd2, MC87; "The Indian War!" *Avant Courier*, September 20, 1877.

338. Crow Scrapbook Collection at Billings Public Library, Billings, Montana.

339. Thackeray, "Counting"; author communication with the late Crow historian Elias Goes Ahead, September 10, 2014.

340. For more on the flight of the Nez Perce, see Jerome Greene, *Nez Perce Summer, 1877* (Helena: Montana Historical Society Press, 2000).

341. Yates to Ruggles, September 22, 1878; Frost to Colonel Buell, September 22, 1878, MF 75, r3.
342. Colonel Miles to War Department, Washington City, July 1, 1878, MF 75, r.3.
343. Ibid.
344. Ibid.
345. Ibid.
346. Miles, *Personal Recollections*, 285.
347. Ibid., 295.
348. Ibid.
349. Ibid., 296.
350. "Letter from Crow Agency," *Helena Weekly Herald*, September 12, 1878.
351. Miles, *Personal Recollections*, 294–300; Brown, *Plainsmen of the Yellowstone*, 319; "Letter," *Helena Weekly*, September 12, 1878; "The Battle of Clark's Fork," *Helena Weekly Herald*, September 19, 1878; Augustus Keller to Ezra Hayt, CIA, December 9, 1879, Bx1/Fd2, MC87.
352. Brown, *Plainsmen*, 320; *Helena Weekly*, September 19, 1878; Keller to Hayt, December 9, 1879. A fund was taken up at the agency for the benefit of his wife; Keller to R.E. Trowbridge, CIA, October 1, 1880; December 9, 1879, Bx1/Fd3 MC87.

6. Annuities, Inspectors and Fraud

353. Kappler, *Indian Affairs*, 2:1008–12.
354. E.M. Camp to Viall, August (no date), 1870, ARCIA.
355. Pease to Viall, August 31, 1871, ARCIA.
356. Slim Jim, "From the Crow Agency," *Avant Courier*, April 4, 1872.
357. Uknow, "From Crow Agency," *Avant Courier*, November 12, 1875.
358. Frost to Smith, August 8, 1877, r506-NA234.
359. "The Mountain Crows," *Helena Weekly Herald*, December 20, 1877.
360. "The Crow Indians," *Avant Courier*, December 26, 1878.
361. Ibid.
362. Marquis, *Custer, Cavalry and Crows*, 130.
363. Marquis, *Memoirs of a White Crow*, 57.
364. Lynna Smith, "Crow Indians Early Reservation Period Oral History Project," Extreme History Project, May 1, 2015, https://www.youtube.com/watch?v=oJ788dr20HI.
365. Ibid.

366. Old Horn, "Crow River and Place Names," February 4, 2021, https://m.facebook.com/LBHCLibraryArchives/videos/dale-old-horn-on-crow-river-and-place-names/141122071175945/.

367. Prucha, *Great Father*, 192.

368. Ibid.

369. Phillips, "Indian Ring in Dakota Territory," 1–25.

370. Ibid., 345.

371. Cohen, *Handbook of Federal Indian Law*, 11.

372. Prucha, *American Indian Policy in Crisis*, 33.

373. Ibid., 40.

374. *Cree Report*.

375. Prucha, *Great Father*, 193.

376. Chandler, *Report of Secretary*, 663.

377. Marquis, *Memoirs of a White Crow*, 59–60.

378. Brown, *Plainsmen of the Yellowstone*, 436.

379. Captain Ball to Hayt, February 18, 1878, Brisbin Papers, Bx/Fd1.

380. Ibid.

381. Ibid.

382. Frost to Hayt, October 21, 1877, Bk1/Fd1, MC87.

383. Russell, *Treasure State Tycoon*, 121–48; Alegria and Fulton, "Fraud," 63–66; Frost to Hayt, CIA, October 31, 1877, Bk1/Fd1, MC87.

384. Russell, *Treasure State Tycoon*, 121–48.

385. Meikle, "No Paper Trail," 78; "Ex-Indian Agent Frost," *Helena Weekly Herald*, November 6, 1879.

386. "A Letter from David Kern, ESQ," *Avant Courier*, October 10, 1878.

387. "The New Agent," *Avant Courier*, November 21, 1878.

7. Agent Augustus Keller

388. Agent Augustus Rufus Keller to E.A. Hayt, CIA, December 26, 1878, MF 75, r3.

389. William P. Clark report, November 27, 1878; Major James Brisbin report, December 10, 1878; Keller to Hayt, December 26, 1878, MF 75, r3.

390. Keller to Hayt, April 26, 1879, MF 75, r3.

391. Samuel Word to Carl Schurz, MF 75, r3.

392. Keller to Hayt, April 26, 1879, MF 75, r3.

393. Keller to Hayt, March 11, 1879, MF 75, r3.

394. Crow council report, April 23, 1879, MF 75, r3.

395. Ibid.
396. Ibid.
397. Crow council report, May 16, 1879, MF 75, r3.
398. Crow council report, April 23, 1879, MF 75, r3.
399. Crow council report, March 8, 1879, MF 75, r3.
400. Ibid.
401. Ibid.
402. Ibid.
403. Ibid.
404. Keller to Hayt, July 3, 1879, RG 75, r3.
405. Keller to Hayt, February 23, 1880, Bx1/Fd2, MC87.
406. Keller to Rowland E. Trowbridge, CIA, Feb 23, 1880, Bx1,/Fd2, MC87.
407. Statistics found in ARCIA, 1880, 166–67.
408. Medicine Crow, *Counting Coup*, 17–26.
409. Keller to Hiram Price, CIA, May 28, 1881, May 27 to July 4, 1881, Corr. MSUB.
410. Charles Barstow Crow council report, March 23, 1880, Bx1/Fd2, MC87.
411. Barstow to General Ruger, April 30, 1880, via February census count, Bx1/Fd2, MC87.
412. Barstow report, March 23, 1880.
413. Ibid.
414. Hoxie, *Parading Through History*, 117.
415. Barstow report.
416. Ibid.
417. Keller to Hayt, December 30, 1879, Bx1/Fd2, MC87.
418. Ibid.; Keller to Trowbridge, CIA, August 12, 1880, Bx1/Fd3, MC87.
419. Keller to Hayt, July 29, 1879, ARCIA.
420. Keller to Hayt, December30, 1879, Bx1/Fd2, MC87.
421. Martin Maginnis to Trowbridge, January 14, 1880, Special Case 52 Crow Agency.
422. Barstow report, March 23, 1880.
423. Ibid.
424. Ibid.
425. Hoxie, *Parading Through History*, 117–18.
426. Barstow report, March 23, 1880.
427. Barstow to Captain Erasmus C. Gilbreath, March 26, 1880, Bx1/Fd2, MC87.
428. *Evening Star* (Washington, D.C.), March 22, 1880.
429. Nabokov, *Native American Testimony*, 177.
430. Ibid., 178.

431. Ibid.

432. Ibid., 179.

433. Ibid., 176–78; Heidenreich, "Crow Delegation," 54–67.

434. Crow council report, June 12, 1880, Bx1/Fd3, MC87.

435. *Evening Star* (Washington D.C.), April 13, 1880.

436. Tim McCleary notes, "War Honor Insignia," to author, September 8, 2020.

437. *Star*, April 13, 1880.

438. "Entertaining the Indians," *Evening Star* (Washington, D.C.), April 23, 1880.

439. Ibid.

440. Crow council report, June 12, 1880.

441. Nabokov, *Native American Testimony*, 181.

442. Ibid., 181.

443. Barstow to Thin Belly, April 16, 1880, Bx1/Fd2, MC87.

444. Barstow to Tom Kent, April 19, 1880, Bx1/Fd2, MC87.

445. Barstow to Nelson Story, May 17, 1880, Bx1/Fd2, MC87.

446. Barstow to T.C. Power, May 11, 1880, Bx1/Fd2, MC87.

447. Barstow to Power, May 29, 1880, 1880, Bx1/Fd2, MC87.

448. Ibid.

449. Barstow to Trowbridge, April 1, 1880, Bk1/Fd2, MC87; Keller to Trowbridge, August 12, 1880, Bx1/Fd3, MC87. No disrespect intended.

450. Barstow to Keller, April 1,1880, Bx1/Fd2/MC87; Barstow to Trowbridge, April 1, 1880, Bx1/Fd2, MC87.

451. Barstow to Keller, April 1, 1880: Barstow to Trowbridge, April 1, 1880.

452. Barstow to Keller, May 31, 1880, Bx1/Fd2, MC87.

453. Barstow to Keller, June 3, 1880, Bx1/Fd2, MC87.

454. Council report, June 12, 1880, Bx1/Fd3, MC87.

455. Ibid.

456. Ibid.

457. The Treaty of 1880, ratified April 11, 1882, available at http://lib.lbhc.edu/index.php?q=node/199.

458. Brown, *Plainsmen of the Yellowstone*, 357; Bradley, "After the Buffalo Days," 97.

459. Hoxie, *Parading Through History*, 119–20.

460. Carl Schurz to Keller, September 27, 1880, Bx1/Fd3, MC87.

461. Keller to Trowbridge, October 4, 1880; October 22, 1880, Bx1/Fd3, MC87.

462. Telegram to Keller, October 6, 1880, Bx1/Fd3, MC87.

463. Bradley, "After the Buffalo Days," 98–99; Smith, "Politics and the Crow," 33.

464. Council report, May 26, 1881, May 6 to May 26, 1881, Corr. MSUB; Keller to Inspector William J. Pollock, May 30, 1881, May 6 to May 26, 1881, Corr. MSUB.

465. Council report, May 26, 1881.
466. Ibid.
467. Ibid.
468. Council report, June 18 1881; May 27 to July 4, 1881, Corr. MSUB.
469. *Columbus News*, January 18, 1923.
470. S. Exec. Doc. No. 61, 10, 15.
471. Ibid., 12-13.
472. Ibid., 17.
473. Ibid., 17–22.
474. Ibid., 13; "Through the Crow Reserve," *Avant Courier*, August 25, 1881.
475. Council report, July 19, 1881, July 16 to July 25, 1881, Corr. MSUB.
476. Keller to Hiram Price, August 13, 1881, Bx1/Fd4, MC87.
477. Samuel J. Kirkwood, SecInt to Robert S. Gardner, Inspector November 21, 1881, Bx1/Fd4, MC87.
478. Keller to Colonel G.K. Sanderson, December 15, 1881, Bx1/Fd 4, MC87.
479. Keller to R.S. Gardner, Inspector, December 15, 1881, Bx/Fd 4, MC87.

8. *Agent Henry J. Armstrong*

480. Agent Henry Armstrong to Hiram Price, CIA, January 31, 1882, January 9–February 12, 1882, Corr. MSUB.
481. Ibid.
482. Armstrong to Price, March 2, 1882, February 14–March 13, 1882, Corr. MSUB.
483. Armstrong, January 31, 1882.
484. Armstrong to Price, February 10, 1882, January 9–February 12, Corr. MSUB.
485. Armstrong to Price, June 1, 1882, May 26–June 8, 1882, Corr. MSUB.
486. Armstrong to Price, March 24, 1882, March 16–April 6, 1882, Corr. MSUB.
487. Armstrong, June 1, 1882.
488. Armstrong to Price, May 12, 1883, Bx1/Fd5 MC87.
489. Armstrong, June 1, 1882.
490. Armstrong to Price, July 24, 1882, July 6–July 27, 1882, Corr. MSUB.
491. F.M.W., "Jottings of a Wanderer," *Helena Weekly Herald*, July 13, 1882.
492. Ibid.
493. Hoxie, *Parading Through History*, 17, 20.
494. Armstrong to Price, December 6, 1882, WhiteBear Pease Collection, 351–60.
495. Armstrong to Price, January 31, 1883, Bk1/Fd5, MC87.

496. Armstrong, August 15, 1883, ARCIA.

497. Armstrong, January 31, 1882.

498. Utley, *Indian Frontier*, 229–30.

499. Linderman, *Pretty Shield*, 76–79.

500. Brink, *Imagining Head Smashed In*, 27.

501. Roscoe, "Life and Times," 47, 50.

502. McCleary, *Crow Indian Rock Art*, 23.

503. Armstrong to Price, March 31, 1883 Bk1/Fd5, MC87; Hoxie, *Parading Through History*, 113. This death was reported multiple ways as Crazy Head's brother, as his son and as his brother-in-law.

504. Hoxie, *Parading Through History*, 113.

505. Armstrong to Price, March 9, March 31, April 6, 1883, Bk1/Fd5, MC87; Hoxie, *Parading Through History*, 20; "Fear an Outbreak of Crows," *River Press* (Fort Benton, MT), August 9, 1883; "Mont Stock Growers Convention," *Rocky Mountain Husbandman* (Diamond City), August 7, 1884.

506. Armstrong to Price, March 9, 1883, Bk1/Fd5, MC87.

507. Ibid.

508. Ibid.

509. Armstrong to Price, May 8, 1883, Bk1/Fd5, MC87.

510. Armstrong to Price, May 22, 1883, Bk1/Fd5, MC87.

511. Armstrong to Price, May 12, 1883 Bk1/Fd5, MC87.

512. Senate Report 283, 6.

513. Ibid.

514. Ibid., 23.

515. Armstrong to Price, June 1, 1882, May 26–June 8, 1882, Corr. MSUB.

516. Armstrong, August 15, 1883, ARCIA.

517. Armstrong report, September 2, 1882, ARCIA.

518. Ibid.

519. Armstrong to Price, June 13, 1883, Bk1/Fd5, MC87.

520. Armstrong report, September 2, 1882.

521. Armstrong to Price, March 24, 1882, March 16–April 6, 1882, Corr. MSUB.

522. Armstrong, March 24, 1882.

523. Armstrong to Price, June 30, 1882, June 13–July 5, 1882, Corr. MSUB.

524. Little Big Horn College, "Place Name," http://lib.lbhc.edu/index.php?q=node/200&a=B.

525. Dr. Thomas B. Marquis, "Recollections of "A White Crow Indian;" The Late Thomas Leforge Speaks From Notes. Was Present at Golden Spike Ceremony," *Billings Gazette*, February 14, 1932.

526. Lindau, "Across Montana," 60–65.

527. Barstow Scrapbook.

528. Armstrong to Price, February 24, 1884, February 13–April 30, 1884, Corr. MSUB.

529. Armstrong to Price, March 8, 1884, February 13–April 30 1884, Corr. MSUB.

530. Armstrong to Price, August 31, 1884, ARCIA.

531. Armstrong to Price, May 5, 1884, May 2–May 15, 1884, Corr. MSUB.

532. *Daily Enterprise* (Livingston, MT), April 7, 1884.

533. Armstrong to Price, May 5, 1884, May 2–May 15, 1884, Corr. MSUB.

534. Armstrong to Barstow, April 28, 1884, February 15–April 30, 1884, Corr. MSUB.

535. Armstrong to J.C. Wilson, April 30, 1884, February 15–April 30, 1884, Corr. MSUB.

536. Armstrong to Price, August 31, 1884, ARCIA.

537. Annin, *They Gazed*, 2:129.

538. Armstrong, August 31, 1884.

539. Ibid.

540. Senate Report 283, 2.

541. Armstrong to Price, May 13, 1884, May 2–May 15, 1884, Corr. MSUB.

542. *Daily Enterprise*, July 11, 1884.

9. Education

543. Wright to E.P. Smith, CIA, March 11, 1873, r496-NA234.

544. Marquis, *Memoirs of a White Crow*, 40.

545. Wright to Smith, May 28, 1874, r500-NA234.

546. Wright, May 28, 1874.

547. Marquis, *Memoirs of a White Crow*, 40.

548. Wright to Smith, February 21, 1874, r500-NA234.

549. Wright to Smith, May 28, 1874, r500-NA234.

550. Wright, May 28, 1874.

551. Armstrong to Price, June 39, 1882, June 13, 1882 to July 5, 1882, Corr. MSUB.

552. Wright to Smith, May 9, 1874, r.500-NA234; Wright to Smith, September 21, 1874, ARCIA.

553. Keller to E.M. Marble acting CIA, August 12, 1880, ARCIA.

554. Frost to Hayt, August 20, 1878, ARCIA.

555. Armstrong to Price, June 30, 1882, June 13–July 5, 1882, Corr. MSUB

556. Camp to Sully, August (no date) 1870, ARCIA.

557. *Fourth Report*, 86.
558. Frost to Hayt, August 20, 1878, ARCIA.
559. Keller to Hayt, July 29, 1879, ARCIA.
560. Pease to E.P. Smith, September 28, 1873, ARCIA.
561. Blackfoot to President Grant, December 5, 1873, r500-NA234.
562. Keller to Marble, August 12, 1880, ARCIA.
563. Keller to Hayt, July 29, 1879, ARCIA.
564. Frost to Hayt, August 20, 1878, ARCIA.
565. *Seventh Annual Report*, 8.
566. Prucha, *American Indian Policy in Crisis*, 271–74.
567. Keller to Trowbridge, October 11, 1880, Bk1/Fd 3, MC87.
568. Armstrong to Price, February 18, 1882, January 9–February 12, 1882, Corr. MSUB.
569. Armstrong, February 18, 1882.
570. Armstrong to Price, May 4, 1882, May 4–May 23, 1882, Corr. MSUB.
571. Armstrong to Price, February 8, 1883, Bk1/Fd5, MC87.
572. Armstrong to Price, February 22, 1883, Bk1/Fd5, MC87.
573. *The School News*, Carlisle Barracks, March 1883, vol. 111, number 10.
574. Student descriptive https://carlisleindian.dickinson.edu/sites/default/files/docs-documents/NARA_RG75_91_b0164_21545_0.pdf.

10. *A Look into the Absaroka Agency*

575. Annin, *They Gazed*, 2:131.
576. Clapp to E.P. Smith, September 27, 1875, RG 75.
577. U Know, "From the New Crow Agency," *Avant Courier*, July 9, 1875.
578. "The New Agency," *Avant Courier*, July 30, 1875.
579. Bradley, *March of the Montana*, 38.
580. Fred Wilson, "The Crow Indians," *Avant Courier*, December 26, 1878.
581. Ibid.
582. Allen, "Building of Crow Indian Agency."
583. U Know, "From the Crow Agency," *Avant Courier*, December 31, 1875.
584. F.M.W., "Jottings of a Wanderer," *Helena Weekly Herald*, July 13, 1882.
585. Clapp to Smith, August 31, 1875, RG 75.
586. "Colonel Tells of Early Days," *Columbus News*, April 12, 1928.
587. Clapp to Smith, September 10, 1875, RG 75.
588. Allen, "Building of Crow Indian Agency."
589. Clapp, September 10, 1875.

590. F.M.W., "Jottings."

591. *Bozeman Weekly Chronicle*, August 8, 1883.

592. No disrespect intended.

593. Hallock, "Sketches of the Yellowstone Country," MSU-Bozeman.

594. Crow files at Museum of the Beartooths.

595. Armstrong to Price, May 13, 1884, Corr. MSUB.

596. September 20, 1885, Armstrong, ARCIA.

597. Statistics in 1883 and 1884, ARCIA.

598. Stan Stephens, "Crow Oral History Project 1," Extreme History Project, October 1, 2014, https://www.youtube.com/watch?v=FN3848TMETc.

599. The $46,000 figure was for the purchase of 2,500 head of cattle as negotiated by Plenty Coups. The annuity fund was reduced by $200,000 in the new agreement and applied to irrigation funding.

600. Hoxie, *Parading Through History*, 231; Crow Agreement of 1891; http://lib.lbhc.edu/about-the-crow-people/government-and-law/agreement-of-1891.php.

601. Smith, "Politics and the Crow," 34; ARCIA, June 30, 1901, 54.

602. For in-depth chronicling, see Hoxie, *Parading Through History*, chapter 9.

BIBLIOGRAPHY

Collections

Barstow, Charles H. Scrapbook; MSU, Bozeman, MT. Special Collections.

Brisbin, James Papers, Coll.39, Bx/Fd No. 1. Montana Historical Society (MHS).

Carlisle School records. https://carlisleindian.dickinson.edu

Crow Agency General Correspondence, Special Collections Montana State University-Billings [hereafter, Corr. MSUB]. Marquis, Thomas binder, Big Horn County Museum, Hardin, MT.

Record Books of Crow Indian Agency, 1877–1894, (RCIA)-MC87. MHS.

Special Case 52, Crow Agency, MHS.

U.S. Office of Indian Affairs, Letters Received, National Archives and Records Administration, Washington D.C. 1824–1880, (NA234).

U.S. Office of Indian Affairs, Montana Superintendency Records, 1825–1880, MF 75 MHS (3 rolls of microfilm). MHS.

WhiteBear, Eloise, and Pease Collection, Little Big Horn College.

Books

Albright, Peggy. *Crow Indian Photographer, The Works of Richard Throssel.* Albuquerque: University of New Mexico, 1997.

Algier, Keith. *The Crow and the Eagle: A Tribal History from Lewis and Clark to Custer.* Caldwell, ID: Caxton Printers, 1993.

Annin, Jim. *They Gazed on the Beartooths*. 3 vols. Billings, MT: Artcraft Printers, 1964.

Bourke, John G. *On the Border with Crook*. New York: Charles Scribner's Sons, 1891.

Bradley, James H. (James Howard). *The March of the Montana Column: A Prelude to the Custer Disaster*. Edited by Edgar I. Stewart. Norman: University of Oklahoma Press, 1961.

Brink, Jack W. *Imagining Head Smashed In: Aboriginal Buffalo Hunting on the Northern Plains*. Edmonton, AB: Athabasca University Press, 2017.

Brown, Mark H. *The Plainsmen of the Yellowstone*. New York: G.P. Putman, 1961.

Cohen, F.S. *Handbook of Federal Indian Law: With Reference Tables and Index*. Washington, D.C.: U.S. Government Printing Office, 1942.

Curtis, Edward. *The North American Indian*. Vol. 4, *The Apsaroke, or Crows. The Hidatsa*. Cambridge, MA: University Press, 1904. https://dc.library.northwestern.edu/items/6b144fb9-8b01-45ff-a53d-2b5bb610240d.

Finerty, John F. *War-Path and Bivouac, The Big Horn and Yellowstone Expedition*. Edited by Milo Milton Quaife. Chicago: R.R. Donnelley, 1955.

Gray, John S. *Centennial Campaign, The Great Sioux War of 1876*. Norman: University of Oklahoma Press, 1988.

———. *Custer's Last Campaign, Mitch Boyer and the Little Bighorn Reconstructed*. Lincoln: University of Nebraska Press, 1991.

Green, Jerome. *Nez Perce Summer, 1877, The U.S. Army and the Nee-Me-Poo Crisis*. Helena: Montana Historical Society Press, 2000.

Hoxie, Frederick E. *Parading Through History: The Making of the Crow Nation in America 1805–1935*. Cambridge: Cambridge University Press, 1995.

Hyde, George E. *Red Cloud's Folk: A History of the Oglala Sioux Indians*. Norman: University of Oklahoma Press, 1979.

Kappler Charles J, ed. *Indian Affairs: Laws and Treaties*. Vol. 2, *Treaties*. Washington, D.C.: Government Printing Office, 1904.

Koury, Michael J. *Guarding the Carroll Trail and Camp Lewis, 1874–1875*. Fort Collins, CO: Old Army Press, 1985.

Linderman, Frank B. *Plenty-Coups: Chief of the Crows*. Lincoln: University of Nebraska Press, 2002.

———. *Pretty Shield: Medicine Woman of the Crows*. Lincoln: University of Nebraska Press, 2003.

Lopez, Marty. "Shiipdeetdeesh." In *Apsáalooke Women and Warriors*, edited by Nina Sanders and Dieter Roelstraete, 11. Chicago: Neubauer Collegium, 2020.

Mangum, Neil C. *Battle of the Rosebud: Prelude to the Little Big Horn*. El Segundo, CA: Upton and Sons, 1996.

Marquis, Thomas. *Custer, Cavalry and Crows: The Story of William White*. Fort Collins, CO: Old Army Press, 1975.

———. *Memoirs of a White Crow Indian* (Thomas Leforge). Lincoln: University of Nebraska Press, 1974.

McCleary, Timothy. *Crow Indian Rock Art, Indigenous Perspectives and Interpretations*. Walnut Creek, CA: Left Coast Press, 2016.

———. "A History of the Apsaalooke." In *Apsáalooke Women and Warriors*, edited by Nina Sanders and Dieter Roelstraete, 119–25. Chicago: Neubauer Collegium, 2020.

Medicine Crow, Joseph. *Counting Coup: Becoming a Crow Chief on the Reservation and Beyond*. Washington, D.C.: National Geographic Society, 2006.

———. *From the Heart of Crow Country: The Crow Indians' Own Stories*. New York: Orion Books, 1992.

Meikle, Lyndel. "No Paper Trail: Crooked Agents on the Crow Reservation, 1874–1878." In *Speaking Ill of the Dead, Jerks in Montana*, 68–83. Essex, CT: Globe Pequot, 2011.

Miles, Nelson Appleton. *Personal Recollections and Observations of General Nelson A. Miles*. Chicago: Werner, 1896.

Nabokov, Peter. *Native American Testimony, An Anthology of Indian and White Relations: First Encounter to Dispossession*, New York: Harper, 1978.

———. *Two Leggings: The Making of a Crow Warrior*. New York: Thomas Y. Crowell Co., 1967.

Prucha, Francis Paul. *American Indian Policy in Crisis: Christian Reformers and the Indian, 1865–1900*. Norman: University of Oklahoma Press, 1976.

———. *The Great Father: The United States Government and the American Indians*. Lincoln: University of Nebraska, 1986.

Russell, John C. *Treasure State Tycoon: Nelson Story and the Making of Montana*. Helena: Montana Historical Press, 2019.

Rust, Tom. *Lost Fort Ellis: A Frontier History of Bozeman*. Charleston SC: The History Press, 2015.

Scott, Kim Allen. *Splendid on a Large Scale: The Writings of Hans Peter Gyllembourg Koch*. Helena, MT: Drumlummon, 2010.

Topping, E.S. (Eugene Sayre). *Chronicles of the Yellowstone*. Minneapolis, MN: Ross & Haines, 1968.

Utley, Robert M. *The Indian Frontier of the American West, 1846–1890*. Albuquerque: University of New Mexico Press, 1984.

———. *The Lance and the Shield: The Life and Times of Sitting Bull*. New York: Ballantine Books, 1993.

Viola, Herman J. *Little Bighorn Remembered: The Untold Indian Story of Custer's Last Stand.* New York: Times Books, 1999.

Wyndham-Quin, Thomas Windam. *The Great Divide: Travels in the Upper Yellowstone in the Summer of 1874.* Lincoln: University of Nebraska Press, 1981.

Reports

Chandler, Zachariah. *Report of Secretary of the Interior.* Washington, D.C. Government Printing Office, 1875.

Cree, Thomas. *Fifth Annual Report of the Board of Indian Commissioners to the President of the United States.* Washington, D.C.: Government Printing Office, 1874 [hereafter *Cree Report*].

Fourth Annual Report of the Board of Indians Commissioners of the President of the United States: 1872. Washington, D.C.: Government Printing Office, 1872.

Senate Report 283. "Report of the Select Committee to Examine the Condition of the Sioux and Crow Indians," 48th Congress, 1st Session., Serial 2174. Washington, D.C.: Government Printing Office, 1884.

Seventh Annual Report of the Board of Indian Commissioners. Vol. 7, *1875.* Washington, D.C.: Government Printing Office, 1876.

S. Exec. Doc. No. 61, 47th Congress, 1st Sess. 1882.

Sixth Annual Report of the Board of Indians Commissioners. Vol. 6, *1874.* Washington, D.C.: Government Printing Office, 1875.

United States Congress. *The Congressional Globe.* 42nd Congress, 2nd Session, 1871–72. Washington. D.C.: Blair & Rives, 1834–73.

———. *The Congressional Globe.* 42nd Congress, 3rd Session, 1872–73. Washington, D.C.: Blair & Rives, 1834–73.

United States Office of Indian Affairs. *Annual Report to the Commissioner of Indian Affairs, (ARCIA), 1870–1885.* Washington, D.C.: Government Printing Office, 1902.

Periodicals, Dissertations, Diaries and Manuscripts

Alegria, Crystal, and Marsha Fulton. "Fraud at Fort Parker." *Montana Magazine of History* 66 (Autumn 2016): 51–67.

Allen, Jirah. "Building of Crow Indian Agency Offered Variety of Experiences." *Columbus News*, October 20, 1927.

Big Man, Alden. "Crow History 1700–1950: A Political and Social Battle to Retain Their Culture." PhD dissertation, University of New Mexico, 2011.
———. "Curly the Sole Survivor of Custer's Command." *True West Magazine*, May 1, 2001.

Bradley, Charles C. "After the Buffalo Days: Documents on Crow Indians from the 1880s to 1920s." Master's thesis, Montana State University, 1970.

Bradley, James H. "Bradley Manuscript: Yellowstone Expedition of 1874." Contributions to the Historical Society of Montana, VIIT, Helena, 1917.

Brekke. "Historical Overview of Benson's Landing Park County, Montana." Anthro Research, Inc. Livingston, Montana (January 2007).

Brown, Mark H. "Muddled Men Have Muddied the Yellowstone's True Color." *Montana Magazine of History*, January 1961.

Burlingame, Merrill G. "The Andrew Jackson Hunter Family, Mary Hunter Doane." *Montana Magazine of History*, Winter 1951.

Doyle, Shane. "In Home Land." *Mountain Journal*, November 2019. https://mountainjournal.org.

Hallock, Charles. "Sketches of the Yellowstone Country." *American Field: The Sportsman's Journal*, February 1882.

Heidenreich, Adrian C. "The Crow Delegation to Washington D.C. in 1880." *Montana Magazine of History*, Spring 1981.

Humpherys, Glen A. "The Crow Indian Treaties of 1868, An Example of Power Struggle and Confusion in United States Indian Policy." *Annals of Wyoming* (Spring 1971): 73–88.

Kennedy, Margaret. "Whoop-Up Trail of Northcentral Montana." National Register of Historic Places, 1991.

Libby, Orin G. *The Arikara Narrative of the Hostile Campaign Against the Dakotas, June 1876*. Bismarck: North Dakota Historical Society, Vol. 6, 1920.

Lindau, Paul. "Across Montana on the Northern Pacific in 1883." *Montana Magazine of History*, Spring 1985.

Marquis, Thomas B. *The First Crow Agency*. Big Horn County Museum, Hardin, MT.
———. "Recollections of 'A White Crow Indian': The Late Thomas Leforge Speaks From Notes. Was Present at Golden Spike Ceremony." *Billings Gazette*, February 14, 1932.

McLemore, Clyde, "Fort Pease, The First Attempted Settlement in Yellowstone Valley," Montana Magazine of History, January 1953.

Oman, Kerry R. "The Beginning of the End; The Indian Peace Commission of 1867–1868." *Great Plains Quarterly* 22, no. 1 (Winter 2002): 35–51.

Pease, Fellows D. Diary, Carbon County Historical Society, Red Lodge, MT (CCHS).

Phillips, George H. "The Indian Ring in Dakota Territory, 1870–1890." *South Dakota Historical Society Press* 2 (1972).

Roscoe, Will. "The Life and Times of a Crow Berdache." *Montana Magazine of History*, Winter 1990.

Silliman, Lee. "The Carroll Trail: Utopian Enterprise." *Montana: The Magazine of Western History*, Spring 1974.

Smith, Burton M. "Politics and the Crow Indian Land Cessions." *Montana Magazine of History*, Autumn 1986.

Thackeray, Lorna. "Counting on the Crow." *Billings Gazette*, October 6, 2002.

INDEX

ABOUT THE AUTHOR

Patricia Molinaro, a graduate of the University of Montana, is a self-proclaimed aficionado of western history. She is author of *Columbus and Stillwater County*, *Beartooth Mountains* and *Moccasins, Mining and Montana's 34th County*. She has served as director in two Montana county museums and is presently on the board of Our Montana Inc., an organization promoting and preserving the heritage of Montana. When not researching or writing, Patty enjoys exploring for rock art, historic structures, hiking, riding, photography and working with her registered Angus cattle. Patty is respectful of the fact she resides in the shadow of Crow and Butcher Mountains, lands that once belonged to the Crow peoples. The names of both are linked directly to the tribe and their prior occupation of the area.

Visit us at
www.historypress.com
....